Anti-Inflammatory Cookbook For Lazy People

Paulina .V Noble

It always seems impossible until it's done. - Nelson Mandela

It's definitely a motivational factor, becoming a three-organization world champion. - Benson Henderson

A somebody was once a nobody who wanted to and did. - John Burroughs

Get action. Seize the moment. Man was never intended to become an oyster. - Theodore Roosevelt

Introduction

This cookbook is designed to introduce you to the concept of an anti-inflammatory diet and provide you with delicious and healthy recipes to incorporate into your daily meals. By following an anti-inflammatory diet, you can reduce inflammation in your body and promote overall health and well-being.

The cookbook begins by explaining what the anti-inflammatory diet is all about. You will learn about the principles of this diet, which focuses on consuming whole foods that are known for their anti-inflammatory properties. Understanding the basics of the anti-inflammatory diet will help you make informed choices when selecting ingredients and preparing your meals.

Chronic inflammation is a common health issue that can lead to various symptoms and health risks. The cookbook explores the symptoms of chronic inflammation, helping you recognize potential signs and take action to address them. Additionally, you will learn about the health risks associated with chronic inflammation, emphasizing the importance of managing inflammation through dietary choices.

Common treatments for chronic inflammation are also discussed in the cookbook. While consulting with a healthcare professional is essential for personalized advice, this section provides general information on common treatments and lifestyle changes that can support your anti-inflammatory journey.

One of the key benefits of following an anti-inflammatory diet is its positive impact on your overall health. The cookbook highlights the health benefits associated with an anti-inflammatory diet, such as reducing the risk of chronic diseases, supporting digestion, and promoting a healthy weight. These benefits will motivate and inspire you to embrace the anti-inflammatory lifestyle.

Now let's move on to the recipes! The cookbook features a wide range of recipes organized into different meal categories. You'll find delicious and nutritious options for breakfast, lunch, dinner, fish and seafood, poultry, meat, vegetarian dishes, snacks, and desserts.

The breakfast section offers a variety of options to start your day off right, including flavorful smoothies, spiced oatmeal, egg scrambles, and more. These recipes will give you a healthy and satisfying boost of energy to kick-start your mornings.

For lunch, you'll discover a selection of salads, soups, wraps, and other nutritious dishes. These recipes are designed to be easy to prepare and packed with anti-inflammatory ingredients, making them perfect for a nourishing midday meal.

When it comes to dinner, the cookbook provides a range of options that are both delicious and anti-inflammatory. From hearty stews and stir-fries to flavorful curries and roasted vegetables, you'll find a variety of dishes to suit your taste buds and dietary preferences.

Fish and seafood lovers will find a collection of recipes featuring salmon, shrimp, cod, and more. These recipes showcase the health benefits of incorporating omega-3 fatty acids into your diet.

Poultry recipes offer alternatives for those looking for lean protein options. You'll find flavorful chicken and turkey recipes that are both satisfying and anti-inflammatory.

For meat enthusiasts, the cookbook includes recipes that prioritize lean cuts and incorporate anti-inflammatory ingredients. These recipes will help you enjoy meat while still following the principles of the anti-inflammatory diet.

Vegetarian recipes cater to those who prefer plant-based options. You'll find creative and flavorful recipes that showcase the versatility of vegetables, legumes, and plant-based proteins.

Snacks are an essential part of any diet, and the cookbook offers a variety of healthy and delicious options. From energy bites and veggie chips to hummus and guacamole, these snacks will keep you satisfied and support your anti-inflammatory goals.

Finally, no meal is complete without a sweet treat. The dessert section of the cookbook provides recipes for guilt-free indulgence. From fruity desserts to chocolate treats, you can satisfy your sweet tooth while still staying true to your anti-inflammatory journey.

Each recipe is accompanied by clear instructions and tips to ensure successful preparation. The cookbook emphasizes the use of fresh, whole ingredients and provides alternative options for dietary restrictions or preferences.

Embrace the anti-inflammatory lifestyle and discover the joy of preparing and enjoying meals that nourish your body and support your overall well-being. Get ready to embark on a delicious and healthy culinary journey with this book!

Contents

CHAPTER 1: WHAT IS THE ANTI-INFLAMMATORY DIET?

The anti-inflammatory diet is defined as a specific diet to fight latent inflammations in your body entirely naturally.

In fact, the anti-inflammatory diet essentially has species of natural or vegetable origin as ingredients. In reality, it is not a vegan or vegetarian diet as some products of animal origin are allowed, but always in very moderate quantities and especially in distant moments.

In fact, your first goal will be to have a balanced diet, that is, tailored to your habits and your work, family, and personal activities.

You do not have to overdo the food you introduce in each meal. Still, it is good to spread the quantities (and calories) over several meals or at different times.

Excess calories and their consequent non-disposal cause severe problems for your body, primarily overweight and obesity.

Today these two diseases are one of the leading causes of death in our country, or, in general, they are diseases that lead to other secondary conditions that can cause severe discomfort (such as inflammation) and generate a period of depression.

So, the first step you need to consider is to significantly reduce the calories introduced into your diet and try to have a correct calorie intake, i.e., neither too high nor too low. Next, we will see some practical and straightforward tips for how to do and behave at the table.

Another aspect that needs to be taken care of is eating habits. We are often used to eating out of hours, or when we should have a simple snack, we find ourselves ingesting large portions of a given food. Consequently, our metabolism is compromised.

You will need to determine which eating habits suit your overall health and tailor them to your lifestyle.

With practice and time, you will soon realize that the anti-inflammatory diet is your best ally against inflammation. Hence, the real benefits you will perceive in the concise term. While in the long run, you will notice a strong feeling of positivity and well-being as well as, of course, weight loss and its stabilization. In fact, it is essential not to be fluctuating with weight, that is, not to lose and gain weight in a short time, but it is always better to be constant and have a weight that does not fluctuate too much.

Constant weight will help you reach your health goals first, and then write down what your target weight or ideal weight should be.

I confess to you an important thing. In reality, each individual has their own ideal weight, and it is impossible to generalize values that are the same for everyone. In fact, your perfect weight will fundamentally depend on your life and the activities (work but not only) you carry out every day.

Constantly monitoring your weight is essential, and so is its stabilization.

An anti-inflammatory diet is an excellent tool to stabilize your weight and regain your ideal weight. In fact, the anti-inflammatory diet will allow you to feel good immediately and give yourself (why not) some whim.

Do not waste time with news or miraculous solutions you find on the net; instead, invest a small amount of money in understanding what is right and what is not by talking to an expert.

The anti-inflammatory diet will thus constitute a significant barrier that will hinder the onset of certain disorders, such as inflammation but not only.

We will see later the miraculous role that fiber and all the other natural substances present in plants and in the recipes contained in this book have.

CHAPTER 2: SYMPTOMS OF CHRONIC INFLAMMATION

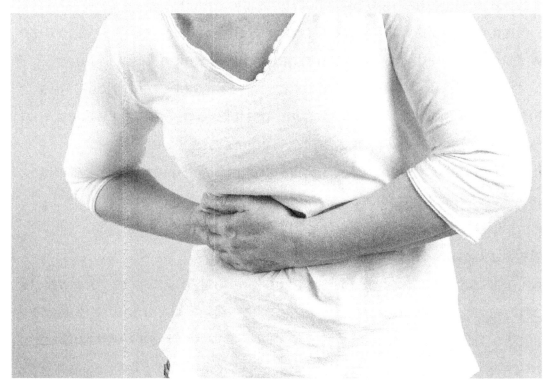

Inflammations of the body are a very complex process and involve many metabolic reactions and can affect multiple parts and organs of the human body.

In fact, in several studies conducted on patients with more or less intense chronic inflammations, the presence of specific protein molecules capable of causing pain in the affected area was found. The molecules in question are cytokines. For some years, it has been discovered that the presence of these molecules is indirectly related to the inflammation of a given organ or tissue. However, their concentration and the perception of pain that comes with it also vary. Consequently, it is impossible to estimate pain based on their attention; however, their presence is intrinsically related to a disorder (or even a disease). Therefore, it is good to take action.

The symptoms that we will now analyze are very variable and depend on the general health of each person. In fact, there is no public indication nor a unique and specific therapy. Instead, each person follows his own healing process, which can be more or less long, depending on the type of inflammation and degree of acuity he possesses.

Inflamed people are also subject to other disorders; therefore, the general clinical picture is more complex.

- **Accumulation of metabolic fluids.** In some parts of the body, there can be actual accumulations of fluids. These liquids are often part of the normal body fluids that cannot "drain" properly; that is, they cannot circulate freely because of an "obstacle." In these situations, one should proceed cautiously by intervening from the outside. Still, often the affected part hurts too much and cannot be touched. You can then try to proceed with targeted physical activity (or stretching) to gradually improve the circulation of liquids. The people most interested in this phenomenon are those who do a sedentary job, obese people, or who have suffered minor traumas (such as childbirth or other interventions).

- **Feeling of general tiredness.** Have you ever tried to perform intense physical activity and couldn't get out of bed the next day? It seems that playing sports can be dangerous. The truth is that practicing sports is really good. Still, it must be done intelligently, and we need to warm up the muscles that interest us. Our forces have been under severe stress when these unpleasant situations occur. They have produced lactic acid (and other secondary metabolites) to naturally counteract the exertion. When we are in the presence of chronic inflammation, the principle is the same. In fact, there are accumulations of organic acids inside the body. As a result, all the muscles close to the affected area are subject to drastic changes and cannot perform natural movements correctly. This is where we feel tiredness and stress when we are inflamed but cannot take any action comes from. In these particular situations, it is tough to force yourself to perform a movement; instead, it is better to rest and try to find relief in the most comfortable position. Food should also be excluded, but better only to drink alkaline water.
- **Sleep disorders.** When we are inflamed, and consequently, some organs and tissues are loaded with

tension, acids, and other metabolites specific to inflammation, we often cannot find a correct and comfortable position, especially during the night hours when we should sleep. As a result, sleep is compromised, and finding the right place is almost impossible. Other times post-meal inflammation can occur (for example, if we ate large quantities of food at dinner), and sleep is not immediately found because our body is still in digestion. Sleeping well is very important to our body, so don't eat large amounts of food before bed.

- **Difficulty losing weight.** When we start a diet or a new path of change, we are motivated to change rhythms and eating styles. However, over 80% of people drop out after the first month. Because? Because it doesn't see actual results. One among them is weight loss. In inflamed subjects, it is difficult to lose weight as there are many fluids (which cannot be disposed of with diet and physical activity alone) but must be drained gradually, which takes time. Often these people also have a different psychological state of health and are, therefore, more sensitive. My advice is not to be disheartened if the results you were hoping for do not arrive but to increase your focus and energy. Weight loss should be a secondary aspect. First, however, it is more important to reduce inflammation and the related disorders that derive from it.

This way, your body works better, and your metabolism is better. Then, later on, you can think about constant weight loss.

- **Mental fatigue.** Mental fatigue is a widespread pathology in our country. The people who suffer from it are often subjects who lead relatively everyday life but cannot find a moment or a space for themselves. As previously mentioned, when chronic inflammation is present in a body, situations that are difficult to manage, like making simple movements or displacements, can occur. In the long run, these difficulties inevitably lead to periods of severe stress and, in some cases, even depression. You have the feeling of being useless and of not being able to do anything. In reality, there is always a solution to all this, and you shouldn't be in a hurry; instead, it is better to be patient and roll up your sleeves. Chronic inflammations cannot be managed by us and are natural defense mechanisms of our body.

- **Headache and headaches.** In more studies, it has been seen and shown that people with inflammation suffer from headaches in 93% of cases. To date, the real cause of headaches is still unknown, but they are often attributed to the person's lifestyle. In fact, people who lead an intense life, full of many appointments and things to do, if they cannot manage their strength, their rest, and their nutrition in the best possible way, inevitably incur more or less severe and painful headaches. Headaches, if poorly managed, can also become disabling, and you can't think of anything. An anti-inflammatory diet is one of your best allies to fight this problem. First, I advise you not too fast for many hours but rather integrate at least one portion of fruit every 3 hours. This way, your brain will always have a few available sugars. Always follow the directions of your doctor.

• **Other minor ailments.** The list of possible diseases and disorders that can cause inflammation is very long, and other minor conditions have been documented several times. However, it is not just the single nuisance that needs to be monitored, but the whole picture of overall health. In fact, often, all these disorders can present themselves more or less intensely in a single subject and trigger significant conditions and confusion about what is best to do and what not. So, for starters, don't try to overdo it but rather start gradually with your diet and healthy habits, such as taking a simple walk or having a good time with your loved ones. Then, you can progressively enter the rest of the advice you will find in this book.

WHAT CAN TRIGGER INFLAMMATION

Now let's see what may be the leading causes that can trigger chronic inflammation within the human body.

Obviously, the indications mentioned here result from a lot of experience and are not random notions. Instead, they have been ascertained by proven studies. Often even the combination of two or more of these phenomena can trigger a single inflammation, or even a single factor can trigger multiple rashes in multiple body parts and of different intensities.

In general, I recommend that you try to lead a quiet and healthy life, do not weigh yourself down with diet, and play sports. Sport produces many benefits for your body and health, even on a mental level. In addition, it allows you to relax, which is not too noticeable.

SMOKING AND ALCOHOL

These two elements often coexist in an inflamed individual. In the literature, several studies show how these two elements alone can cause many inflammations throughout the body without considering the possible cancers that can trigger in the mouth. Lungs, skin, and dementia. Until a few decades ago, our country was among the first in the world to people with problems related to smoking; fortunately, this event has been reduced considerably. However, smoking is terrible and produces severe inflammation.

Alcohol, on the other hand, is one of the main enemies of our body, brain, and immune system. Often, we do not realize it, but we ingest too many quantities of alcohol or hard alcohol in less-than-optimal conditions, i.e., between meals. On these particular occasions, our body struggles to dispose of alcohol. It is slowly eliminated in the urine; if it is taken immediately after meals, its elimination is faster. However, I am not recommending alcohol. Did you know that the energy value of alcohol is 9 kcal, precisely like lipids? However, lipids are digested by our complex metabolic machine, while alcohol is slowly through the kidneys.

It is, therefore, best to avoid abusing these toxic habits, and it is better to prevent the formation of possible tumors or cancers. I assure you that people with these diseases have compromised lives and live badly. Even the people who try to help them live a difficult life of sacrifice and renunciation.

On average, people who do not use alcohol and do not smoke do not get inflamed as quickly and are more resistant to possible stress inflammation or other traumatic events. In other words, they are happier people.

IRRITABLE COLON

Irritable bowel is a very annoying disease. In addition to the intense sensation of abdominal cramps and burning, the irritable bowel irremediably leads to altered metabolism of some substances in our diet.

The drugs used for its treatment can provide temporary relief but not definitively cure the disease. The friendly bacterial flora that lives in the intestine is often profoundly compromised.

Friendly bacteria play a vital role in our body; they produce many substances that are good for the heart, arteries, liver, circulation, and general psychic well-being. However, if these life forms are altered due to the potent drugs taken, all the substances they typically produce are changed or simply not made.

In the colon, fluids are also reabsorbed from the stool, and this is where the stool solidifies. People with irritable bowel can also have frequent episodes of diarrhea for this very reason.

Eating healthy food, not burdening our intestines and friendly bacteria is also fundamental. Inevitably, chronic inflammations are produced if the intestine does not work, which are more or less painful.

Most plants contain fibers that help restore the bacterial flora (the microbiota). So, in the long run, it may return to function properly.

POOR HYGIENE

Personal hygiene is the first element to pay attention to when inflammation occurs. In fact, poor hygiene inevitably leads to the presence of unpleasant odors and the formation of toxic bacteria. As seen above, chronic inflammation can be triggered either by internal factors or other factors such as bacteria or viruses. We now have straightforward weapons within everyone's reach to ensure adequate daily hygiene. We respect our bodies and wash them properly.

EXTREME AND UNCONTROLLED PHYSICAL ACTIVITY

Physical activity is an excellent weapon for losing weight and activating metabolism.

However, often some beginners make the mistake of performing a short period of intense and out-of-control physical activity. In 3 out of 4 cases, unexpected damage can occur to your body as you try too hard and unnecessarily. In fact, most doctors recommend starting daily physical activity, targeted and, above all, not intense.

If you are not a professional athlete, you cannot push your body to the limit to lose weight. Better to exercise every day rather than once every 2 weeks. This way, more calories are consumed, and you feel good every day.

Also, in this case, I would advise you to contact an expert who may follow you in the first movement sessions and not rely on chance.

If you already feel inadequate after the first steps toward weight loss, you will not achieve anything. Instead, you must accustom your body to the change gradually and constantly.

SLEEP DISORDERS

In recent studies, 1 in 3 Americans has been found to suffer from sleep disorders. Many people are now used to taking their pills before going to sleep and not thinking about it anymore. However, if there are disturbances in our restful sleep, we must ask ourselves why they occur. In some cases, they can occur due to a too-high-calorie dinner, because we have been too active, or simply because we look at the television screen or our smartphone.

The phases of sleep are critical and delicate; it is here that our body regenerates and restores the metabolism. Conversely, if it is altered, some metabolic and mental mechanisms are literally changed.

Therefore, it is essential to have a peaceful, long, and restful sleep; in the morning, we should wake up happy and ready to start a new day.

Suppose sleep is compromised on the other hand. In that case, short periods of inflammation can occur first, and then, if neglected, chronic and latent inflammation can occur.

The only advice I would like to give you is to find the proper routine before relaxing and falling asleep. Reading can be a valuable ally and try to fast for at least 3 hours before going to sleep.

CHAPTER 3: HEALTH RISKS OF CHRONIC INFLAMMATION

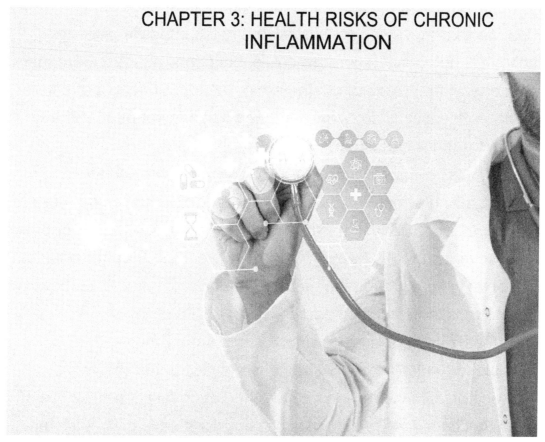

If poorly managed or neglected over time, chronic inflammation can cause a series of problems for our body. It is, therefore, suitable to follow a quiet life, a balanced diet, and, above all perform blood and urine tests periodically (at least once a year). The cost of these tests is relatively low and is often included in some health insurance.

The blood test allows you to fully understand the general health of your body. It will give you an idea if you are experiencing a moment of severe stress or anxiety or if everything is okay.

Some diseases can trigger chronic inflammation, such as rheumatoid arthritis or illnesses related to the intestine. Among these, it is noted that ulcerative colitis and Crohn's disease are the most annoying. In fact, often, the clinical picture of people affected by these diseases is compromised, and episodes of psoriasis and psoriatic arthritis can occur.

This complex clinical picture leads to managing excruciating and often disabling symptoms. Unfortunately, these diseases can also trigger other comorbidities, such as cardiovascular diseases or even more severe cancers. People who suffer live with perennial pain that is difficult to cure. Often, their family members or loved ones have a life compromised by these people.

Unfortunately, there is no cure for every disease. However, it is possible to gradually reduce the pain and discomfort you feel by following precise instructions from your diet. In fact, if the degree of inflammation is not too high, it is possible to literally extinguish the inflammation by feeding on the best or even more suitable food for your situation.

Remember that there is no general menu valid for everyone, but a specific menu must be written for each individual. In fact, each of us has a different metabolic cycle that varies according to gender, age, weight, general health, physical fitness, basal metabolic rate, and professional activity.

So yes, it is correct to say that you can start from a general food context, but then you must follow your own rhythms and habits.

WHAT HAPPENS WHEN CHRONIC INFLAMMATION IS NEGLECTED

Patients suffering from chronic inflammation often have a compromised general clinical picture and poor health status. This means these people are already living with other health and social problems.

When chronic inflammation occurs, small warning signals (pain) are sent. Still, these are often not correctly received by the sick person. When these signals become stronger and more intense, you go to the doctor, but the pathology has already developed.

In many cases, the doctor prescribes drugs to relieve the pain immediately, and we find peace of mind momentarily.

In reality, we should intervene immediately and in-depth.

If chronic inflammation is present, our body is not healthy. Still, it asks us to be more careful about our actions.

Obviously, I am not referring only to diet but also to all other aspects of our life, such as social relationships, physical activity, and even our profession.

In fact, we will see in the next chapter how to best manage and treat chronic inflammation, what doctors recommend and what is helpful to know to start your path right away.

When chronic inflammation is present within the body, specific defense mechanisms have activated that try in every way to counter the burning or discomfort they cause.

As we said earlier, our body produces cytokines. These signal molecules make our brain understand that there is inflammation through pain.

The body's other defense mechanisms are an intense concentration of white blood cells in the affected area and a substantial influx of blood and other fluids to try to oxygenate the inflammation.

If all these natural warning signs are overlooked, the pain increases, and the sensitivity of the affected area is reduced.

These mechanisms may appear strange, but in reality, they are entirely natural. It is necessary to intervene in the shortest possible time and in the best possible way, even with the diet.

Let's now see what the main treatments that are used when chronic inflammation is present are. These general guidelines, however, always rely on what your doctor says and still follow a healthy and peaceful life.

CONTROLLED FEEDING

Having total control over your diet is your first ally. As we said earlier, nutrition is the key to literally extinguishing your chronic inflammation. You will notice the benefits in some cases immediately; in others, it will take longer. However, you will see significant changes starting with your weight, mood, and social relationships.

I, therefore, recommend that you start gradually, perhaps following a weekly menu, and also try to write a diary of what you eat and the time.

Over time you will understand what is best to eat and at what times of the day. Try to avoid eating at night and be regular at mealtimes. If you have a shift work situation, try to prepare your meals at home in advance; in this way, you will not have to eat quickly what you find, but you will know exactly what awaits you.

FAST

Fasting is one of the most potent weapons for restoring metabolism and losing weight. Its operation is effortless: do not eat but drink a lot of water.

The fasting principles are ancient, and recent studies have shown their effectiveness today. In fact, when we stop eating and drink only water, the body, in the first phase (about 3 days), goes into stress and has a strong feeling of tiredness. However, starting from the fourth or fifth day, the body begins to regain energy by literally burning the fats present and with the consequent weight loss.

The metabolism of fatty acids is very complex and occurs when we do not ingest sugar in our diet. Water is also required to digest fats, so you must drink while fasting.

However, fasting shouldn't just be done for weight loss. It's a real journey.

Do not start alone; instead, rely on experts or people who practice it regularly.

To start fasting, you need solid personal motivation, don't start out for fun.

DRINK A LOT OF WATER

Water is an excellent ally for fighting inflammation. We should drink at least 10 cups of water daily, but I recommend you also drink 12 cups.

Not all waters are the same. For example, we are used to drinking tap water that our state sanitizes in advance by adding chlorine (in small quantities) to avoid toxic bacteria.

However, suppose you are considering a particular diet. In that case, you may want to invest a small amount of money for slightly alkaline water with a relatively low fixed residue (<100). In this case, you should read the label of the bottle you have chosen and see if it matches these parameters.

IMPROVE THE QUALITY OF YOUR LIFE

The quality of our life is made up of many things. In fact, in our life, in addition to work, our friendships, our parents or relatives, our travels and activities, sports, and even our nutrition.

All of these factors affect the overall quality of our life. It is, therefore, reasonable to find a natural balance with everything without sacrificing anything. However, if you notice that one of these factors is also altered, work on tweaking and fixing it for the better.

A quality life significantly reduces your inflammation and overall body health.

LOW-INTENSITY SPORTS

As previously mentioned, a sport practiced without control, and high intensity can be deleterious. So, it is best to constantly practice a quiet sport that impacts our metabolism.

Examples are brisk walking, light running, swimming, cycling, and tennis or paddling.

You may develop new habits, such as cycling to work or getting off one stop earlier in your own transport and continuing on foot.

All of these are little habits that will help you find your perfect fitness over time.

ONLY NECESSARY DRUGS

We are now used to taking more or less light drugs every day. As soon as we have a little discomfort or pain, we immediately take the pill.

The problem can often be solved with food or movement (I am referring to temporary ailments, not diseases).

If we reduce the number of unnecessary pills we take, we improve the quality of our nutrition and life. Each drug cures something but inevitably kills another. Check with your doctor to see if you can cut back on any medications and promise yourself that you'll be in better shape in return.

CHAPTER 5: HEALTH BENEFITS OF AN ANTI-INFLAMMATORY DIET

Now let's see the main benefits you can observe by following the indications relating to the anti-inflammatory diet.

When you change your diet, you also change your life and how you approach food. It is, therefore, suitable to consider that profoundly changing your diet affects many aspects of your life, including the social ones.

So don't limit the anti-inflammatory diet to just a short period of the year but expand it throughout your life.

WEIGHT LOSS

You will follow an anti-inflammatory diet more controlled and selected diet. You will also take in more fiber and protein of plant origin and reduce the general consumption of foods of animal origin. This translates into fewer calories entering your body and more fiber, keeping you full immediately when you start your meal.

Weight loss is an almost normal consequence. Remember that losing weight gradually rather than in fits and starts is good.

ELIMINATION OF ACUTE INFLAMMATIONS

Acute inflammations are triggered by sudden and intense stress. Suppose your diet is balanced and rich in polyphenols and healthy substances. In that case, you will notice that acute inflammation occurs only in sporadic cases or even never. This is because your body is ready to fight the substances secreted during inflammation and has the right weapons.

DRASTIC REDUCTION OF CHRONIC INFLAMMATION

Chronic inflammations are more complex metabolic mechanisms that can affect multiple body parts and even various organs.

The anti-inflammatory diet is designed for precisely this type of inflammation. In fact, the aches and pains you feel are slowly reduced until they sometimes disappear.

REDUCES BAD CHOLESTEROL

Cholesterol is an essential molecule in our body and the precursor of certain vital hormones. However, its excessive intake in the diet does not help the body lose weight but instead increases the volume of adipose tissue. The anti-inflammatory diet provides a substantial reduction of foods rich in bad cholesterol. But on the other hand, it encourages the consumption of foods rich in good cholesterol, which is helpful for our bodies.

QUALITY OF LIFE IMPROVEMENT

All these aspects related to your new diet inevitably lead to a continuous and gradual improvement in the overall quality of your life.

When you are more aware of what you eat, and when you are in great shape, your mental state improves and your relationships as well.

OXIDATIVE STRESS

Inflammations often lead to the formation of toxic substances that should be eliminated. Usually, our body has the right weapons to destroy them independently. Still, the anti-inflammatory diet literally gets a boost to eliminate these substances and restore the state of health.

These substances are mainly of natural origin and are polyphenols which, in various studies, can break down the general oxidative stress of the body and make you feel good immediately.

It improves general aging.

In the long run, people who follow the anti-inflammatory diet have experienced incredible aging. Still, at 70, they carry out intense social activities; they get together and live happily. All these are thanks to the substantial benefits that their diet (and their health) provides them every day.

CHAPTER 6: FOODS TO CONSUME OR AVOID

In this chapter, we will see a small list of foods that should always be present in your diet and not be missing in every meal.

FRUITS AND VEGETABLES

Fruits and vegetables are the main foods containing fiber and other natural substances such as vitamins, alkaloids, natural sugars, polyphenols, tannins, etc.

They are excellent foods to snack on and fill you up earlier in a meal.

CEREALS

Cereals are the primary food that allows you to have energy immediately and preserve it even if you have to face a short fasting period. In fact, these contain complex carbohydrates and fiber. The extraordinary thing is that taking a mix of cereals also allows you not to have insulin peaks and to have stable glucose levels over time.

UNPROCESSED FOOD

Unprocessed food is the food that comes closest to natural foods. It is, therefore, better to prefer little or no processed foods rather than complex foods that have undergone many transformations. Unprocessed food is easier to digest and metabolize. Our body wastes no time breaking it down into simpler substances before it can metabolize.

POLYUNSATURATED FATS

Polyunsaturated fats are a natural ally that allows you to keep the health of your heart, veins, arteries, blood system, digestive system, and even the brain stable. They are essential because our body cannot produce them, and they must be taken daily, but without exaggeration. In fact, remember that they are very rich in energy but also in fiber.

They are found mainly in fish and dried fruit such as walnuts, almonds, cashews, and lupins.

LEGUMES

Legumes are a food that should be consumed at least 3 times a week. You can also think about cooking it one day a week and then freezing it so that you don't have to prepare everything every time. They are the wealthiest vegetables in proteins and micronutrients such as iron, potassium, magnesium, and calcium. Their combination can quickly meet the protein needs that meat of animal origin provides.

As for the foods to reduce consumption or eliminate instead, we have:

INDUSTRIALIZED FOODS

Industrialized foods are all foods that have undergone transformation processes with a machine. By far, they are the most caloric, and often they contain a lot of energy and few substances beneficial to our body. So, it is good to drastically reduce their consumption or completely eliminate them from your diet.
If you are starting your anti-inflammatory diet now, you can also think about eliminating them for 1 month. Then, you will immediately notice the positive change you will experience.

EXCESS OF SIMPLE SUGARS

Simple sugars are the main culprits of widespread diseases in our country, such as diabetes (type 2) and obesity. They are also responsible for other severe conditions, such as metabolic syndrome. Their consumption should therefore be reduced if not completely eliminated from the diet.

Suppose you practice a sporting activity at a professional level at some moments of your training. In that case, you should take them in controlled quantities and calibrate them according to your food plan.

SATURATED FATTY ACIDS

Saturated fatty acids are among the most toxic substances you can take and are also the main precursors of inflammation and general metabolic disorders.

Their use should be drastically limited, and if it can be eliminated. They are found in some cuts of meat, in all milk products (cheeses and dairy products), in some artificial plant foods, such as vegan butter (which does not exist in nature), or in all spreadable cheeses. Some fruits also contain saturated fatty acids, such as coconut, which grows in tropical countries where certain climatic conditions exist.

CALORIE FOODS

In general, all foods with a high energy content should be limited. Both for weight loss and for the proper functioning of your body. Calorie foods tend to be tastier and have excellent taste; therefore, it is difficult to limit them. However, if you know exactly what the benefits you can get from a correct and balanced diet are, you can safely eliminate them.

ALCOHOLIC

Alcohol is a severe problem in our society. These are drinks that our body cannot digest properly, and due to the intense volatility of the molecule, alcohol immediately reaches the brain causing many problems.

Alcohol also has a caloric value identical to fatty acids (9 kcal). Consequently, its abuse also causes severe problems with the metabolism, liver, kidneys, and digestion.

Limit or eliminate this substance from your diet to get better immediately.

CHAPTER 6: BREAKFAST

HOME-FRIED BREAKFAST POTATOES

Preparation time: 10-minute **Cooking time:** 20 minute **Servings:** 4
Ingredients:

- 3 tbsp. olive oil
- 5 medium red potatoes, peeled and sliced
- 4 slices of cooked bacon, crumbled
- 1 tsp. salt
- ¾ tsp. ground paprika
- ¼ tsp. ground black pepper

Directions:
In a sizable nonstick skillet, heat 1 tbsp. Of olive oil over medium-high heat. Add olive oil, salt, pepper, paprika, and bacon crumbles. About 20 minutes of cooking time, with occasional turning, should result in tender, browned potatoes. Serve warm.
Nutrition: 342 cals; protein 9.6g; carbs 42.8g; fat 15.6g; chole 13.2mg; sodium 875mg.

APPLE-TAHINI TOAST

Preparation time: 5 minutes **Cooking time**: 0 minutes **Serves:**1
Ingredients:

- 2 slices of whole-wheat bread, toasted
- 2 tablespoons tahini
- 1 small apple of your choice, cored and thinly sliced
- 1 teaspoon honey

Directions:
Spread the tahini on the toasted bread. Place the apple slices on the bread and drizzle with the honey. Serve immediately.
Nutrition: calories: 458 | fat: 17.8g | protein: 11.0g | carbs: 63.5g

OATMEAL COOKIES

Preparation time: 15 minute **Cooking time:** 14 minutes **Servings:** 24

Ingredients:

- 3 ¼ cups of old-fashioned oats, divided
- ½ cup of chopped walnuts
- ⅓ cups of raisins
- 2 tbsp. ground flax seeds
- 1 tsp. ground cinnamon
- ¼ tsp. baking powder
- ¼ tsp. salt
- 2 ripe bananas
- 2 eggs
- ⅓ cups of unsweetened applesauce
- 1 tbsp. honey
- 1 tbsp. vanilla extract

Directions:
Set the oven to 350°F. Use parchment paper to line two baking sheets. To make 2 cups of ground oats, grind 2 1/4 cups of oats in a food processor. Salt, baking powder, cinnamon, walnuts, raisins, and flax seeds can also be added. Add remaining cups of oats and stir. With a spoon, mix well but stop grinding after that. In the middle of the oat mixture, create a well. Add the applesauce, honey, vanilla extract, eggs, and bananas. Combine and then stir in the oat mixture. The cookie dough should be deposited on the baking sheets by tbsp. Fuls. Bake in the oven for 14 minutes or until the edges are golden.

Nutrition: 88 cals; protein 2.6g; carbs 13.3g; fat 3g; chole 15.5mg; sodium 36.5mg.

CHEESY BACON CASSEROLE

Preparation time: 15 minute **Cooking time:** 45 minute **Servings:** 6

Ingredients:

- cooking spray
- 4 slices of bread, crusts removed
- 1 ½ cups of skim milk
- 1 cup of egg substitute
- 1 tbsp. chopped fresh chives
- 6 slices of cooked bacon, crumbled
- 1 cups of Cheddar cheese

Directions:
Cooking spray should be used to coat a 9-inch square baking dish. In the bottom of the baking dish that has been prepared, arrange bread slices in a single layer. In a bowl, combine the milk, egg substitute, and chives; pour over the bread pieces in the prepared baking dish. Add some crumbled bacon on top. Wrap the dish in plastic wrap and chill for eight to twelve hours. The baking dish's plastic wrap should be removed and discarded. Allow the dish to sit at room temperature for about 30 minutes. Set oven to 350° F. For 40 minutes, bake the casserole in a preheated oven. After topping with cheese, bake the casserole for another 5 minutes or more, or until the cheese is melted and the casserole is done.
Nutrition: 177 cals; protein 13.1g; carbs 12g; fat 8.3g; chole 21.4mg; sodium 330.2mg.

MEXICAN-STYLE BREAKFAST CASSEROLE

Preparation time: 15-minute **Cooking time:** 55 minutes **Servings:** 8

Ingredients:

- cooking spray
- 1 medium onion, chopped
- 5 cups of shredded hash brown potatoes
- 3 cups of diced ham
- 2 cups of shredded taco-flavored cheese
- 1 (7 Oz.) can diced green chile peppers
- 8 large eggs
- 1 cup of milk
- 1 cup of sour cream
- 1 tsp. taco seasoning mix, or more to taste
- 1 cup of shredded Mexican blend cheese

Directions:
Set the oven to 350°F. A 9x13-inch pan should be sprayed with cooking oil. After heating a small pan with cooking spray over medium heat, onion is added. About 5 minutes should be enough time to cook and toss the onion until it becomes transparent. Add onions, hash browns, ham, taco-flavored cheese, and chili peppers to a big bowl. The bottom of the pan should be layered. Combine the eggs, milk, sour cream, and taco seasoning in a bowl. Over the hash brown layer, pour. Bake in the oven for 45 to 60 minutes, checking after 5 minutes toward the end or until a knife inserted in the center comes out clean. Spread Mexican cheese on top after taking the dish out of the oven. Return to the oven and bake for another 3

minutes or until the cheese is melted. Before serving, let the plate sit for 5 minutes to set.

Nutrition: 528 cals; protein 29.7g; carbs 24.7g; fat 40.4g; chole 270.6mg; sodium 1393.3mg.

BANANA PANCAKES WITH APRICOTS

Preparation time: 5 minutes **Cooking time:** 10 minutes **Serving:** 8
Ingredients:

- 2 oz of banana flour
- 2 oz + 1 teaspoon of ghee
- 1 avocado
- 1 pinch of salt
- 1 teaspoon of turmeric powder
- 1 cup unsweetened coconut milk
- 5 pitted apricots

Directions:
Combine the banana flour with the salt and turmeric powder. In another bowl, combine the 50 grams of ghee with the peeled and pitted avocado and mash with a fork. Combine the two preparations and add the coconut milk slowly, stirring constantly. Spread the dough with a ladle on a baking sheet covered with parchment paper, forming circles. Bake in a hot oven at 360° F for about 10 minutes. While the pancakes are cooking, cut the apricots into cubes and brown them for 5 minutes in a pan with a teaspoon of ghee. Serve pancakes with the apricot compote.
Nutrition: calories: 129 / fat: 11 / protein: 1 / carbs: 10 /

PUDDING WITH BLACKCURRANT AND MINT

Preparation time: 3 minutes + 1 night rest **Cooking time:** 5 minutes **Serving:** 4
Ingredients:

- 1 cup unsweetened coconut milk
- 2 tablespoons of ground Chia seeds
- 1 teaspoon of vanilla extract
- 1 pinch of salt
- 1 cup of blackcurrant
- 2 teaspoons of raw honey
- 5 fresh mint leaves
- 2 tablespoons of water

Directions:
Combine the almond milk with the chia seeds, and add the vanilla extract and salt. Pour the mixture into small glasses and let it rest in the refrigerator overnight. In the morning, mix the honey with the water and put it in a nonstick pan with the currants, cook for 5 minutes. Pour the cooked currants over the puddings, which will have thickened overnight, decorate with mint leaves, and enjoy.
Nutrition: calories: 85 / fat: 3 / protein: 3 / carbs: 15 /

QUINOA BREAD WITH PECAN WALNUT BUTTER

Preparation time: 15 minutes **Cooking time:** 30 minutes **Serving:** 15

Ingredients:

- 1 lb of pecan nuts with pellicle
- 7 oz of hazelnuts
- 6 drops of sage essential oil for food (or 1 tablespoon of sage powder)
- 1 lb of quinoa flour
- 1 dose of organic dry yeast
- 1 + 1/3 cup of water
- 2 tablespoons of olive oil

Directions:
Place the pecans, hazelnuts, salt, and sage essential oil in the blender, after lightly toasting them in the oven at 350° F for 5 minutes. Continue to blend until the nuts release their natural oil, blend until creamy, and add water if necessary. Sage essential oil has a purifying power. If you don't have it, replace it with powdered sage. The bread: mix the quinoa flour with the organic yeast and salt. Slowly add the oil and incorporate the water, preferably lukewarm, into the mixture. Work it with your hands until you get a smooth ball. Let it rise for at least 3 hours in a dark place, sheltered from drafts and warm. Bake in a hot oven at 360° F for about 30 minutes. This bread is very dry and crunchy, perfect for nut butter. Nut butter can be stored in an airtight food container in the refrigerator for at least a week.
Nutrition: calories: 144 / fat: 4 / protein: 5 / carbs: 22 /

OAT FLAKES WITH PEARS AND BLUEBERRIES

Preparation time: 3 minutes **Cooking time:** 10 minutes **Serving:** 2
Ingredients:

- 2/3 cup of rolled oats
- 2 cups unsweetened almond milk
- 1 pinch of salt
- 1/4 cup of blueberries
- 1 pear
- 1 teaspoon of ground cinnamon
- 1 teaspoon of ground ginger
- 1 teaspoon of powdered mint

Directions:
Bring the almond milk, salt, cinnamon, ginger, and mint to a boil in a saucepan. Lower the heat to a minimum and add the oats, cook for about 10 minutes. Serve the oats with fresh blueberries and pear. If you prefer a hot meal, heat the blueberries and pear in a teaspoon of ghee.
Nutrition: calories: 166 / fat: 5 / protein: 5 / carbs: 27 /

SOY CREAM WITH ASPARAGUS

Preparation time: 3 minutes **Cooking time:** 10 minutes **Serving:** 3
Ingredients:

- 1 cup unsweetened natural soy yogurt
- 2 tablespoons of ground flaxseed
- 1 teaspoon of coconut oil
- 11 oz of asparagus
- 1 pinch of salt

Directions:
Cook the asparagus in the steamer. If you do not have the steamer, boil the asparagus in a pan of lightly salted water for 10 minutes. Drain them well and cut them into small pieces. Put the yogurt in a bowl, add the ground flax seeds and mix well. Add the asparagus and season with the olive oil.
Nutrition: calories: 156 / fat: 11 / protein: 8 / carbs: 10 /

SWEET POTATO HASH

Preparation Time: 10 minutes **Cooking Time:** 20 minutes **Serve:** 6
Ingredients:

- 3 cups sweet potatoes, peeled & shredded
- ½ tsp ground nutmeg
- 1 tsp ground cinnamon
- 2 tbsp olive oil
- 1 onion, chopped
- Pepper
- Salt

Directions:
Mix shredded sweet potatoes, onion, cinnamon, nutmeg, pepper, and salt in a mixing bowl. Heat olive oil in a pan over medium heat. Add sweet potato mixture into the pan and cook over medium-low heat. Flip occasionally and cook until lightly brown from all sides, about 20-25 minutes. Serve and enjoy.
Nutrition: Calories 138 Fat 4.9 g Carbohydrates 23 g Sugar 1.2 g Protein 1.4 g Cholesterol 0 mg

SALMON EGG SCRAMBLED

Preparation Time: 10 minutes **Cooking Time:** 8 minutes **Serve:** 2
Ingredients:

- 4 eggs
- 2 tbsp unsweetened almond milk
- 4 smoked salmon slices, chopped
- 1 tbsp olive oil
- 1 tbsp fresh chives, chopped
- Pepper
- Salt

Directions:
Heat olive oil in a pan over medium heat. Whisk eggs with milk, chives, pepper, and salt in a bowl. Pour the egg mixture into the pan and cook over medium-low heat. Stir constantly. When eggs start to set, add salmon slices and cook for 1-2 minutes. Serve and enjoy.
Nutrition: Calories 388 Fat 23.3 g Carbohydrates 0.9 g Sugar 0.7 g Protein 42.3 g Cholesterol 366 mg

CHIA CHOCOLATE PUDDING

Preparation Time: 10 minutes **Cooking Time:** 5 minutes **Serve:** 2
Ingredients:

- 3 tbsp cocoa powder
- 1 cup water
- 1 tbsp honey
- 1 tbsp orange zest
- ¼ cup orange juice
- 1/3 cup chia seeds

Directions:
Add orange juice, zest, honey, water, cocoa powder, and chia seeds into the glass jar and stir until well combined. Cover jar with lid and place in the fridge overnight. Stir well and serve.
Nutrition: Calories 90 Fat 2.6 g Carbohydrates 19.1 g Sugar 11.4 g Protein 2.5 g Cholesterol 0 mg

BAKED OATMEAL

Preparation Time: 10 minutes **Cooking Time:** 30 minutes **Serve:** 6
Ingredients:

- 2 eggs
- ¼ cup raisins
- 1 ½ tsp cinnamon
- 1 tsp baking powder
- ¼ cup oat bran
- 1 ¾ cup rolled oats
- 1 cup unsweetened almond milk
- 1 ½ tsp vanilla
- 2 tbsp fresh turmeric, grated
- 1 ripe banana
- ½ tsp salt

Directions:
Preheat the oven to 350 F. Spray the 8*8-inch baking dish with cooking spray and set aside. Whisk eggs with milk, vanilla, and turmeric until well combined in a bowl. Mix oats, cinnamon, baking powder, oat bran, raisins, and salt in a mixing bowl. Pour egg mixture into the oat mixture and stir until well combined. Pour the oat mixture into the prepared baking dish and bake in preheated oven for 30 minutes. Remove from the oven and let it cool completely. Slice and serve.
Nutrition: Calories 170 Fat 4 g Carbohydrates 28.8 g Sugar 6.7 g Protein 5.9 g Cholesterol 55 mg

CREAMY SMOOTHIE BOWL

Preparation Time: 10 minutes **Cooking Time**: 5 minutes **Serve:** 2
Ingredients:

- ¾ cup oats
- ¼ tsp cinnamon
- 2 bananas, peeled
- 1 ½ tbsp cashew butter
- ¼ cup yogurt
- 1 ½ tsp turmeric
- 2 tbsp walnuts, chopped
- 1 tsp chia seeds

Directions:
Add oats, turmeric, yogurt, cashew butter, bananas, and cinnamon into the blender and blend until smooth. Pour the blended mixture into the serving bowls. Top with walnuts and chia seeds. Serve and enjoy.
Nutrition: Calories 298 Fat 7 g Carbohydrates 52 g Sugar 17 g Protein 9 g Cholesterol 2 mg

MEDITERRANEAN EGGS

Preparation time: 5 minutes **Cooking time:** 20 minutes **Serves:** 4
Ingredients:

- 2 tablespoons extra-virgin olive oil
- 1 cup chopped shallots
- 1 teaspoon garlic powder
- 1 cup finely diced potato
- 1 cup chopped red bell peppers
- ¼ cup chopped fresh cilantro
- 1 (14.5-ounce/ 411-g) can of diced tomatoes, drained
- ¼ teaspoon ground cardamom
- ¼ teaspoon paprika
- ¼ teaspoon turmeric
- 4 large eggs

Directions:
Preheat the oven to 350ºF. Heat the olive oil in an ovenproof skillet over medium-high heat until it shimmers. Add the shallots and sauté for about 3 minutes, occasionally stirring, until fragrant. Fold in the garlic powder, potato, and bell peppers and stir to combine. Cover and cook for 10 minutes, stirring frequently. Add the tomatoes, cardamon, paprika, and turmeric, and mix well. When the mixture bubbles, remove from the heat and crack the eggs into the skillet. Transfer the skillet to the preheated oven and bake for 5 to 10 minutes until the egg whites are set and the yolks are cooked to your liking. Remove from the oven and garnish with the cilantro before serving.
Nutrition: calories: 223 | fat: 11.8g | protein: 9.1g | carbs: 19.5g

CAULIFLOWER BREAKFAST PORRIDGE

Preparation time: 5 minutes **Cooking time:** 5 minutes **Serves:** 2
Ingredients:

- 2 cups riced cauliflower
- ¾ cup unsweetened almond milk
- 4 tablespoons extra-virgin olive oil, divided
- 2 teaspoons grated fresh orange peel (from ½ orange)
- ½ teaspoon almond extract or vanilla extract
- ½ teaspoon ground cinnamon
- ⅛ teaspoon salt
- 4 tablespoons chopped walnuts, divided
- 1 to 2 teaspoons maple syrup (optional)

Directions:
Place the riced cauliflower, almond milk, 2 tablespoons of olive oil, orange peel, almond extract, cinnamon, and salt in a medium saucepan. Stir to incorporate and bring the mixture to a boil over medium-high heat, stirring. Remove from the heat and add 2 tablespoons of chopped walnuts and maple syrup (if desired). Stir again and divide the porridge into bowls. Sprinkle each bowl evenly with the remaining 2 tablespoons of walnuts and olive oil.
Nutrition: calories: 381 | fat: 37.8g | protein: 5.2g | carbs: 10.9g

ALMOND FLOUR PANCAKES WITH STRAWBERRIES

Preparation time: 5 minutes **Cooking time:** 15 minutes **Serves:** 4
Ingredients:

- 1 cup plus 2 tablespoons unsweetened almond milk
- 1 cup almond flour
- 2 large eggs, whisked
- ⅓ cup honey
- 1 teaspoon baking soda
- ¼ teaspoon salt
- 2 tablespoons extra-virgin olive oil
- 1 cup sliced strawberries

Directions:
Combine the almond milk, almond flour, whisked eggs, honey, baking soda, and salt in a large bowl and whisk to incorporate. Heat the olive oil in a large skillet over medium-high heat. Make the

pancakes: Pour ⅓ cup of batter into the hot skillet and swirl the pan, so the batter covers the bottom evenly. Cook for 2 to 3 minutes until the pancake turns golden brown around the edges. Gently flip the pancake with a spatula and cook for 2 to 3 minutes until cooked. Repeat with the remaining batter. Serve the pancakes with the sliced strawberries on top.
Nutrition: calories: 298 | fat: 11.7g | protein: 11.8g | carbs: 34.8g

PISTACHIO AND PECAN WALNUTS GRANOLA

Preparation time: 10 minutes **Cooking time:** 10 minutes **Servings:** 13

Ingredients:

- 1 lb of oat flakes
- 7 oz of dried figs
- 1/2 cup of coconut water
- 7 oz of cashews
- 7 oz of pecans with pellicle
- 1 pinch of salt
- 1 teaspoon ground cinnamon
- 1 teaspoon of raw cocoa powder

Directions:

Blend the dried figs with the coconut water in the food processor. Coarsely chops the pecans and cashew nuts. Mix the cashews, pecans, date paste, cinnamon, salt and cocoa in a bowl. Heat the oven to 350° F. Line a baking sheet with parchment paper. Pour the granola onto the pan, bake for 5 minutes, mix and bake for another 5 minutes. This preparation is excellent in the morning with yogurt or to enrich ice cream and puddings.

Nutrition: Calories: 259kcal; Fat: 19g; Protein: 5g; Carbs: 22g

BANANA MUFFIN

Preparation time: 5 minutes **Cooking time:** 20 minutes **Servings:** 8

Ingredients:

- 2 bananas
- 5 oz of wholemeal flour
- 2 tablespoons of applesauce
- 1 tablespoon of ground chia seeds
- 2 tablespoons of maple syrup
- 2 cups of coconut milk
- 2 tablespoons of coconut butter
- half a sachet of organic baking powder
- 1 pinch of salt

Directions:

Soak the ground chia seeds with 3 tablespoons of water. In a bowl, mix the apple sauce, the soaked chia seeds, the salt, the milk, and the butter. Combine the sifted flour and baking powder, and mix again. Blend the bananas in a mixer and incorporate them into the mixture. Fill the muffin tins to three-quarters of their capacity and bake in a hot oven at 350° F for about 15-20 minutes.

Nutrition:: Calories: 116kcal; Fat: 4g; Protein: 2g; Carbs: 18g

MUSHROOM FRITTATA

Preparation time: 15 minutes **Cooking time:** 20 minutes **Servings:** 6

Ingredients:

- 1½ cups chickpea flour
- 1½ cups water
- 1 teaspoon salt
- 2 tablespoons extra-virgin olive oil
- 1 small red onion, diced
- 2 pints of sliced mushrooms
- 1 teaspoon ground turmeric
- ½ teaspoon ground cumin
- 1 teaspoon salt
- ½ teaspoon black pepper
- 2 tablespoons fresh parsley, chopped

Directions:

At 350°F, preheat your oven. In a suitable bowl, slowly whisk the water into the chickpea flour; add the salt and set aside. Add olive oil to a suitable cast-iron or oven-safe skillet over high heat. When the oil is hot, add the onion. Sauté the onion for 3 to 5 minutes or until the onion, is softened and slightly translucent. Add the mushrooms and sauté for 5 minutes more. Add the turmeric, cumin, salt, and pepper, and sauté for 1 minute. Pour the batter over the vegetables and sprinkle with the parsley. Place the prepared skillet in the preheated oven and bake for 20 to 25 minutes. Serve warm or at room temperature.

Nutrition: Calories: 240kcal; Fat: 7.9g; Protein: 11.4g; Carbs: 33.5g

SPICY QUINOA

Preparation time: 10 minutes Cooking time: 20 minutes Servings: 4

Ingredients:

- 1 cup quinoa, rinsed
- 2 cups water
- ½ cup shredded coconut
- ¼ cup hemp seeds
- 2 tablespoons flaxseed
- 1 teaspoon ground cinnamon
- 1 teaspoon vanilla extract
- 1 pinch salt
- 1 cup fresh berries of your choice
- ¼ cup chopped hazelnuts

Directions:

In a suitable saucepan over high heat, combine the quinoa and water. Bring to a boil, reduce its heat to a simmer, and cook for 15 to 20 minutes until the quinoa is cooked. Stir in the coconut, hemp seeds, flaxseed, cinnamon, vanilla, and salt. Divide the cooked quinoa among into four bowls and top each serving with ¼ cup of berries and 1 tablespoon of hazelnuts.

Nutrition: Calories: 264kcal; Fat: 10g; Protein: 8g; Carbs: 35.4g

TOFU SCRAMBLE

Preparation time: 10 minutes **Cooking time:** 8 minutes **Servings**: 4
Ingredients:

- 3 tablespoons extra-virgin olive oil
- 3 green onions, sliced
- 3 garlic cloves, peeled and sliced
- 1 15-oz package of firm tofu, drained and diced
- Kosher salt, to taste
- 1 cup mung bean sprouts
- 2 tablespoons mint, chopped
- 2 tablespoons parsley, chopped
- 1 tablespoon lime juice
- Fish sauce for serving
- Cooked brown rice for serving

Directions:
Mix olive oil, white parts of the green onions, and garlic in the cold sauté pan. Turn the heat to low. As the aromatics warm, occasionally stir for almost 4 minutes. Add the tofu and salt and reduce its heat to medium. Cook, occasionally stirring, until the tofu is well coated with the oil and warmed for 3 minutes. Add mung bean sprouts and cook for 1 minute. Stir in the green parts of the green onions, mint, parsley, and lime juice. Stir to combine. Taste, adding fish sauce or additional lime juice if desired. Serve the scramble on its own or with poached eggs on brown rice.
Nutrition: Calories: 185kcal; Fat: 14.9g; Protein: 11.1g; Carbs: 5.6g

ANTI-INFLAMMATORY PORRIDGE

Preparation time: 10 minutes   **Cooking time:** 25 minutes   **Servings:** 2

Ingredients:

- ¾ cup Almond Milk, unsweetened
- 2 tbsp. Hemp Seeds
- 2 tbsp. Chia Seeds, whole
- ¼ cup Walnuts, halved
- ¼ cup Almond Butter
- ¼ cup Coconut Flakes, unsweetened & toasted
- ¼ cup Coconut Milk
- ½ tsp. Turmeric Powder
- Dash of Black Pepper, grounded, as needed
- ½ tsp. Cinnamon
- 1 tbsp. Extra Virgin Olive Oil

Directions:

To start with, heat a large saucepan over medium heat. To this, put in the hemp seeds, flaked coconut, and chopped walnuts. Roast for 2 minutes or until toasted. Once the coconut-seed mixture is roasted, transfer to a bowl and set it aside. Then, heat almond milk and coconut milk in a wide saucepan over medium heat. Once it becomes hot but not boiling, remove from the heat. Stir in almond butter and coconut oil to it. Mix. Now, add chia seeds, pepper powder, turmeric powder, and salt to the milk. Combine. Keep it aside for 5 minutes, and then add half of the roasted coconut mixture. Mix. Finally, transfer to a serving bowl and top with the remaining coconut mixture. Serve immediately.

Nutrition: Calories: 575Kcal; Protein: 14.8g; Carbohydrates: 6g; Fat: 50.2g

GINGERBREAD OATMEAL

Preparation time: 10 minutes **Cooking time:** 30 minutes **Servings:** 4

Ingredients:

- ¼ tsp. Cardamom, grounded
- 1/8 tsp. Nutmeg
- 4 cups Water
- ¼ tsp. Allspice
- 1 cup Steel Cut Oats
- 1 ½ tbsp. Cinnamon, grounded
- ¼ tsp. Ginger, grounded
- ¼ tsp. Coriander, grounded
- Maple Syrup, if desired
- ¼ tsp. Cloves

Directions:

Place all ingredients in a huge saucepan over medium-high heat and stir well. Next, cook them for 6 to 7 minutes or until cooked. Once finished, add the maple syrup. Top it with dried fruits of your choice if desired. Serve it hot or cold.

Nutrition: Calories: 175Kcal; Protein: 6g; Carbohydrates: 32g; Fat: 32g

ROASTED ALMONDS

Preparation time: 5 minutes   **Cooking time:** 10 minutes   **Servings:** 32
Ingredients:

- 2 cups whole almonds
- 1 tbs. chili powder
- ½ tsp. ground cinnamon
- ½ tsp. ground cumin
- ½ tsp. ground coriander
- Salt and freshly ground black pepper, to taste
- 1 tbs. extra-virgin organic olive oil

Directions:
Preheat the oven to 350° F. Line a baking dish with a parchment paper. In a bowl, add all ingredients and toss to coat well. Transfer the almond mixture into prepared baking dish in a single layer. Roast for around 10 minutes, flipping twice inside the middle way. Remove from oven and make aside to cool down the completely before serving.
Nutrition: Calories: 62Kcal; Protein: 2g; Carbohydrates: 12g; Fat: 5g

ROASTED PUMPKIN SEEDS

Preparation time: 10 minutes **Cooking time:** 20 minutes **Servings:** 4

Ingredients:

- 1 cup pumpkin seeds, washed, and dried
- 2 tsp. garam masala
- 1/3 tsp. red chili powder
- ¼ tsp. ground turmeric
- Salt, to taste
- 3 tbsp. coconut oil, meted
- ½ tbs. fresh lemon juice

Directions:
Preheat the oven to 350°F. In a bowl, add all ingredients except lemon juice and toss to coat well. Transfer the almond mixture right into a baking sheet. Roast approximately twenty or so minutes, flipping occasionally. Remove from oven and make aside to cool completely before serving. Drizzle with freshly squeezed lemon juice and serve.

Nutrition: Calories: 136Kcal; Protein: 25g; Carbohydrates: 15g; Fat: 4g

QUICK BURRITO

Preparation time: 10 minutes **Cooking time:** 11 minutes **Servings:** 1

Ingredients:

- 1/4-pound beef meat; ground
- 1 tsp. sweet paprika
- 1 tsp. cumin; ground
- 1 tsp. onion powder
- 1 small red onion; julienned
- 3 eggs
- 1 tsp. coconut oil
- 1 tsp. garlic powder
- 1 tsp. cilantro; chopped.
- Salt and black pepper to the taste.

Directions:

Heat up a pan over medium heat; add beef and brown for a few minutes. Add salt, pepper, cumin, garlic, and onion powder and paprika; stir, cook for 4 minutes more, and take off heat.Using a bowl, mix the eggs with salt and pepper and whisk well. Heat a pan with the oil over medium heat; add egg, spread evenly and cook for 6 minutes Transfer your egg burrito to a plate, divide beef mix, add onion and cilantro, roll and serve

Nutrition: Calories: 280Kcal; Protein: 14g; Carbohydrates: 7g; Fat: 5g

NUTTY CHOCO-NANA PANCAKES

Preparation time: 5 Minutes **Cooking time:** 0 Minutes **Serving:** 2
Ingredients:

- 2 eggs
- 2 bananas
- 2 tablespoons creamy almond butter
- 1/8 teaspoon salt
- 2 tablespoons cacao powder
- Coconut oil
- 1 teaspoon pure vanilla extract Sauce:
- 1/4 cup coconut oil
- 4 tablespoons cacao powder

Direction:
Get a pan ready on low heat. Grease the pan with 1 tablespoon of coconut oil. Put everything you need to make pancakes into a food processor. Mix the ingredients and pulse them on high until the batter is completely smooth. To create one pancake, pour approximately a quarter cup of the mixture onto the hot skillet. Flip each pancake after 5 minutes of cooking. Turn the pancake over very gently. For a further 2 minutes, flip the meat. Repeat this process until no more batter is available. Sauce may be served alongside or on the pancakes. Warm the coconut oil in a pan over medium heat. Add the cacao powder to the oil and stir until combined. Get out of the sun. Leave aside.
Nutrition: Calories: 621 Kcal, Proteins: 22.4g, Fat: 32g, Carbohydrates: 66g

BLUEBERRY AVOCADO CHOCOLATE MUFFINS

Preparation time: 15 Minutes **Cooking time:** 0 Minutes **Serving:** 2
Ingredients

- 1/2 cup almond milk (unsweetened)
- 1 cup almond flour
- 1/3 cup coconut sugar
- 1/4 cup cacao powder + 1 tablespoon (raw)
- 1/4 cup blueberries (fresh)
- 2 large eggs (room temperature)
- 1 small avocado (ripe)
- 1/4 teaspoon salt
- 2 tablespoons coconut flour
- 2 teaspoons baking powder
- 2 tablespoons dark chocolate chips

Direction:
Bake at 375° Fahrenheit, which requires preheating the oven. Put paper muffin cups in a muffin tray. Put the eggs, salt, avocados, sugar, and 1 tbsp of the cacao powder in a blender and mix until smooth. The texture should resemble smooth pudding after being blended on high. Put everything in a big basin and stir it up. Sift the cocoa powder, baking soda, almond flour, and coconut flour into a large mixing basin. Combine the ingredients well. Combine the avocado and almond milk and stir to combine. Whisk together the flour and salt in a separate bowl, then add it to the avocado combination and fold until everything is incorporated. Don't beat the mixture to death. Blend in the blueberries and chocolate chips. Spoon the mixture equally into the 9 prepared muffin cups. Put in

the oven and cook for approximately 18 minutes. Do not eat the muffins too warm.

Nutrition: Calories: 130 Kcal, Proteins: 10.4g, Fat: 5g, Carbohydrates: 11g

CHAPTER 7: LUNCH

ANTI-INFLAMMATORY BEEF MEATBALLS

Preparation time: 10 Minutes **Cooking time:** 10 Minutes **Serving:** 4

Ingredients

- 1/4 cup chopped cilantro (tightly packed)
- 2 pounds of ground beef
- 1/2 teaspoon ground ginger
- Zest of 1 lime
- 1/2 teaspoon sea salt
- 5 garlic cloves (pressed)

Direction:

Turn on the oven and set the temperature to 350° F. Put parchment paper on a baking sheet. Put everything you need in a basin and mix it. Maintain a healthy blend. Make 12 meatballs from the mixture. Line a baking sheet with foil and distribute the meatballs on it. Put it in the oven and set the timer for 25 minutes. You may garnish the meatballs with fresh herbs and avocado slices.

Nutrition: Calories: 57 Kcal, Proteins: 4g, Fat: 7g, Carbohydrates: 3g

SALMON WITH VEGGIES SHEET PAN

Preparation time: 25 Minutes **Cooking time:** 30 Minutes **Serving:** 4

Ingredients

- 16 ounces bag of baby potatoes
- 1 teaspoon fresh thyme
- 16 ounces Brussels sprouts (halved)
- 4 6-ounce salmon fillets (skin on)
- 1 cup cherry tomatoes
- 1/2 red onion (cubed)
- 1 bunch of asparagus (trimmed and halved)
- 3 tablespoons balsamic vinegar
- 1 garlic clove (minced)
- 2 tablespoons honey
- 1 tablespoon Dijon mustard
- 2 tablespoons olive oil
- 1/2 teaspoon sea salt

Instructions:

Prepare a 450° F oven temperature. Prepare parchment paper on a baking pan. To make the dressing, combine the vinegar, garlic, honey, Dijon mustard, thyme, and salt in a bowl. Maintain a healthy blend. Asparagus, red onion, Brussels sprouts, potatoes, tomatoes, olive oil, and Three tbsp. The balsamic honey combination should be combined in a separate bowl. Maintain a healthy blend. Prepare a baking sheet by spreading the veggies equally over it. Put in the oven for 10 minutes. The range is done, so remove it. Salmon fillets should be arranged atop the veggies. It's skin-side down. Apply the remaining balsamic honey mixture to each fillet by brushing it on. The baking sheet should be returned to the oven. Put in the oven for 10 minutes. For the next four minutes, broil on high. The fillets' exposed surfaces will brown in this manner. Serve.

Nutrition: Calories: 377 Kcal, Proteins: 38g, Fat: 10g, Carbohydrates: 39g

ROASTED SALMON GARLIC AND BROCCOLI

Preparation time: 25 Minutes **Cooking time:** 35 Minutes **Serving:** 4

Ingredients

- 1 lemon
- 1 1/2 pounds salmon fillets
- 1 large broccoli head
- 2 1/2 tablespoons coconut oil
- 3/4 teaspoon sea salt
- 2 cloves fresh garlic
- Black pepper

Direction:

Prepare a 450° F oven temperature. Put parchment paper on a baking sheet. Put the salmon in an even layer on the prepared baking sheet. There has to be breathing room between the various components. A teaspoon of olive oil should be used to finish cooking the salmon. Distribute the garlic cloves in a thin layer over the fish. Add ½ of the salt and enough pepper to taste. Place a lemon slice atop each serving of fish. Putting aside. Place the broccoli florets, remaining pepper, salt, and 1 1/2 teaspoons of oil in a mixing basin and toss to combine. Toss. Florets should be placed between each slice of salmon. Put the dish in the oven, and set the timer for fifteen min. Parsley and lemon wedges make a lovely garnish. Serve.

Nutrition: Calories: 366 Kcal, Proteins: 35g, Fat: 14g, Carbohydrates: 29g

ROASTED SWEET POTATOES WITH AVOCADO DIP

Preparation time: 25 Minutes **Cooking time:** 40 Minutes **Serving:** 4

Ingredients

- 1 avocado
- 2 large sweet potatoes
- 1 lime (juice)
- 4 tablespoons water
- 1 large clove of garlic (peeled and chopped)
- 1/2 teaspoon sea salt
- 1 teaspoon olive oil
- 2 tablespoons olive oil

Direction:
Turn the oven temperature up to 400° F. Use parchment paper to line a baking sheet. Place the diced potatoes in an equal layer on the prepared baking sheet. Use 2 tbsp of olive oil to drizzle. To ensure that all potato pieces get a coating of fat, you should turn them over. Use a third of the salt for seasoning. Put it in the oven for 40-45 minutes or until it's golden brown. Put the avocados, garlic, lime juice, and the remaining ½ of the salt in a blender and mix until smooth. Combine until the point of smoothness. Stir in the olive oil and the water gradually. Make sure everything is well combined by continuing to blend. Prepare a dip to accompany the cooked potatoes and serve.

Nutrition: Calories: 188 Kcal, Proteins: 3g, Fat: 13g, Carbohydrates: 20g

CHICKEN WITH LEMON AND ASPARAGUS

Preparation time: 15 Minutes **Cooking time:** 20 Minutes **Serving:** 4

Ingredients:

- 2 cups asparagus
- 1 pound of chicken breasts (boneless and skinless)
- 1/4 cup flour
- 2 lemons (sliced)
- 4 tablespoons butter (divided)
- 1 teaspoon lemon pepper seasoning
- 1/2 teaspoon salt
- 1/2 teaspoon pepper

Direction:

Lemons and Asparagus:
The remaining butter should be melted in the same pan over moderate heat. Pour in the asparagus. Heat until the vegetables are crisp-tender. Remove from the stove. Place the lemon slices in a single layer on the hot skillet. Caramelization is achieved by cooking for a few minutes on each side without stirring. Remove from the stovetop.

Chicken: Cut each chicken chest in half lengthwise to make slices that are just 3/4 of an inch thick. Put the flour, salt, and pepper into a wide, shallow dish. Combine harmoniously. Sprinkle the flour mixture over each piece of chicken. Prepare the first ½ of the butter by melting it in a pan over medium heat. Place the chicken pieces within. To get a golden brown color, cook for Five minutes for each side. While cooking, season both sides of the chicken using lime pepper. Putting aside. Assembly: Arrange the cooked asparagus, lemon, and chicken on a serving plate. Serve.

Nutrition: Calories: 250 Kcal, Proteins: 13g, Fat: 7g, Carbohydrates: 26g

APPLE SQUASH SOUP

Preparation Time: 10 minutes **Cooking Time:** 6 hours **Serve:** 8
Ingredients:

- 1 butternut squash, peeled, seeded & diced
- 1 apple, cored and diced
- 2 garlic cloves, minced
- 2 cups vegetable stock
- 1/2 cup can use coconut milk
- 1/8 tsp ground cinnamon
- 1/8 tsp cayenne
- 1 onion, diced
- 1 carrot, peeled and diced
- Pepper
- Salt

Directions:
Add butternut squash and remaining ingredients into the slow cooker and stir well. Cover and cook on low for 6 hours. Puree the soup using a blender until smooth. Serve and enjoy.
Nutrition: Calories 62 Fat 3.1 g Carbohydrates 8.9 g Sugar 4.4 g Protein 0.9 g Cholesterol 0 mg

QUICK PUMPKIN SOUP

Preparation Time: 10 minutes **Cooking Time:** 6 minutes **Serve:** 6
Ingredients:

- 2 cups pumpkin puree
- 1 onion, chopped
- 4 cups vegetable broth
- 1/4 tsp nutmeg
- 1/4 cup red bell pepper, chopped
- 1/8 tsp thyme, dried
- 1/2 tsp salt

Directions:
Stir in the pumpkin puree and the remaining ingredients in the instant pot. Cook on high pressure for 6 minutes, covered. Allow for a 5-minute natural release before releasing any remaining pressure with a quick release. Remove the lid. Using a blender, puree the soup until smooth. Serve immediately and enjoy.
Nutrition: Calories 63 Fat 1.2 g Carbohydrates 9.4 g Sugar 4.2 g Protein 4.4 g Cholesterol 0 mg

CHICKEN SQUASH SOUP

Preparation Time: 10 minutes **Cooking Time:** 25 minutes **Serve:** 4
Ingredients:

- 1 1/4 lbs butternut squash, cubed
- 2 cups cooked chicken, shredded
- 1 cup coconut milk
- 1 tsp garlic, crushed
- 1 leek, sliced
- 1 carrot, chopped
- 1 onion, chopped
- 1 tbsp olive oil
- 3 cups chicken broth
- 1 1/2 tbsp curry powder
- 1 tsp ginger, grated
- Pepper
- Salt

Directions:
Add oil into the instant pot duo crisp and set the pot on sauté mode.
Add ginger, garlic, leek, carrot, and onion, and sauté for 5 minutes.
Add remaining ingredients except for chicken and milk and stir well.
Cover and cook on high pressure for 15 minutes. Once done,
release tension using quick release. Remove lid. Puree the soup
using a blender until smooth. Stir in coconut milk and chicken. Set
pot on sauté mode and cook for 5 minutes. Serve and enjoy.
Nutrition: Calories 407 Fat 21.6 g Carbohydrates 29.7 g Sugar 8.5
g Protein 27.9 g Cholesterol 54 mg

HEALTHY BROCCOLI SOUP

Preparation Time: 10 minutes **Cooking Time:** 3 hours **Serve:** 6
Ingredients:

- 8 cups broccoli florets
- 2 tbsp olive oil
- 6 cups vegetable stock
- 1 tbsp olive oil
- 2 tbsp ginger, chopped
- 4 cups leeks, chopped
- 1 tsp turmeric
- 1/8 tsp pepper
- 1 tsp salt

Directions:
Add broccoli and remaining ingredients into the crockpot and stir well. Cover and cook on low for 3 hours. Puree the soup using a blender until smooth. Season with pepper and salt. Serve and enjoy.
Nutrition: Calories 151 Fat 7.8 g Carbohydrates 18.9 g Sugar 5.1 g Protein 4.9 g Cholesterol 0 mg

ASIAN CHICKEN COCONUT SOUP

Preparation Time: 10 minutes **Cooking Time:** 9 minutes **Serve:** 4
Ingredients:

- 2 lbs chicken breast, boneless & cut into cubes
- 3 cups chicken broth
- 1 red bell pepper, cut into strips
- 2 tbsp Thai curry paste
- 2 tbsp fresh lime juice
- 1 cup coconut milk
- 2 tbsp olive oil
- 2 tbsp fish sauce
- 1 small onion, quartered
- Pepper & Salt

Directions:
Add oil into the instant pot and set the pot on sauté mode. Add onion and cook for 2-3 minutes. Add remaining ingredients except for lime juice and milk and stir well. Cover and cook on high pressure for 6 minutes. Once done, release the pressure manually and remove the lid. Stir in coconut milk and lime juice. Serve and enjoy.
Nutrition: Calories 518 Fat 28.1 g Carbohydrates 11.6 g Sugar 6 g Protein 54.1 g Cholesterol 145 mg

MASHED GRAPE TOMATO PIZZAS

Preparation time: 10 minutes **Cooking time:** 20 minutes **Serves:** 6
Ingredients:

- 3 cups grape tomatoes, halved
- 1 teaspoon chopped fresh thyme leaves
- 2 garlic cloves, minced
- ¼ teaspoon kosher salt
- ¼ teaspoon freshly ground black pepper
- 1 tablespoon extra-virgin olive oil
- ¾ cup shredded Parmesan cheese
- 6 whole-wheat pita breads

Directions:
Preheat the oven to 425°F. Combine the tomatoes, thyme, garlic, salt, ground black pepper, and olive oil in a baking pan. Roast in the preheated oven for 20 minutes. Remove the pan from the oven, mash the tomatoes with a spatula, and stir to mix well halfway through the cooking time. Meanwhile, divide and spread the cheese over each pita bread, then place the bread in a separate baking pan and roast in the oven for 5 minutes or until golden brown and the cheese melts. Transfer the pita bread onto a large plate, then top with the roasted, mashed tomatoes. Serve immediately.
Nutrition: calories: 140 | fat: 5.1g | protein: 6.2g | carbs: 16.9g

GREEK VEGETABLE SALAD PITA

Preparation time: 10 minutes **Cooking time:** 0 minutes **Serves:** 4
Ingredients:

- ½ cup baby spinach leaves
- ½ small red onion, thinly sliced
- ½ small cucumber, deseeded and chopped
- 1 tomato, chopped
- 1 cup chopped romaine lettuce
- 1 tablespoon extra-virgin olive oil
- ½ tablespoon red wine vinegar
- 1 teaspoon Dijon mustard
- 1 tablespoon crumbled feta cheese
- Sea salt and freshly ground pepper, to taste
- 1 whole-wheat pita

Directions:
Combine all the ingredients in a large bowl except for the pita. Toss to mix well. Stuff the pita with the salad, then serve immediately.
Nutrition: calories: 137 | fat: 8.1g | protein: 3.1g | carbs: 14.3g

BURGERS

Preparation time: 1 hour 20 minutes **Cooking time:** 30 minutes
Serves: 6
Ingredients:

- 1 tablespoon avocado oil
- 1 yellow onion, diced
- ½ cup shredded carrots
- 4 garlic cloves, halved
- 1 (15 ounces / 425 g) can of black beans, rinsed and drained
- 1 cup gluten-free rolled oats
- ¼ cup oil-packed sun-dried tomatoes, drained and chopped
- ½ cup sunflower seeds, toasted
- 1 teaspoon chili powder
- 1 teaspoon paprika
- ½ cup fresh parsley stems removed
- ¼ teaspoon ground red pepper flakes
- ¾ teaspoon sea salt
- ¼ teaspoon ground black pepper
- ¼ cup olive oil

For Serving:

- 6 whole-wheat buns, halved and toasted
- 2 ripe avocados, cut

- 1 cup mung bean sprouts or kaiware sprouts
- 1 tomato, peeled and sliced
- 1 teaspoon cumin powder

Directions:

Using parchment paper, line a baking sheet. In a nonstick skillet over medium heat, heat 1 tablespoon avocado oil. Sauté the onion and carrots for 10 minutes, or until the onion has caramelized. Sauté the garlic for 30 seconds, or until fragrant. Add the remaining ingredients, except the olive oil, to a food processor and process until smooth. Pulse until the mixture is finely chopped and holds together. Make certain that the mixture is not puréed. Divide the mixture into six 4-inch-diameter, 12-inch-thick patties. Wrap the baking sheet in plastic wrap after placing the patties on it. Place the baking sheet in the freezer for at least an hour, or until firm.Remove the baking sheet from the fridge and set it aside for 10 minutes to come to room temperature. In a nonstick skillet over medium-high heat, heat the olive oil until it shimmers. Fry the patties for 15 minutes in the skillet, or until lightly browned and crispy. Halfway through the cooking time, flip the patties. To avoid overcrowding, you may need to work in batches. To make the burgers, layer the buns with patties, avocados, sprouts, and tomato slices.

Nutrition: calories: 612 | fat: 21.1g | protein: 26.g | carbs: 88.3g

BROWN RICE WITH BELL PEPPERS

Preparation time: 10 minutes **Cooking time:** 10 minutes **Servings:** 4

Ingredients:

- 2 tablespoons extra-virgin olive oil
- 1 red bell pepper, chopped
- 1 green bell pepper, chopped
- 1 onion, chopped
- 2 cups cooked brown rice
- 2 tablespoons low-sodium soy sauce

Directions:
Heat the olive oil in a large nonstick skillet over medium-high heat until it shimmers. Add bell peppers and onion. Cook for about 7 minutes, until brown. Add the rice and the soy sauce. Cook for about 3 minutes, until the rice warms through.

Nutrition: Calories: 266kcal; Fat: 8g; Protein: 5g; Carbs: 44g

BEAN AND RICE CASSEROLE

Preparation time: 10 minutes **Cooking time:** 35 minutes **Servings:** 4

Ingredients:

- 1 cup soaked black beans
- 2 cups water
- 2 teaspoons onion powder
- 2 teaspoons chili powder, optional
- 2 cups brown rice
- 6 ounces (170 g) tomato paste
- 1 teaspoon minced garlic
- 1 teaspoon sea salt

Directions:

Combine all of the ingredients in your Instant Pot. Choose the "Manual" setting and seal the lid. Cook for 35 minutes under high pressure. Once the cooking is complete, let the pressure release for 5 minutes. Then perform a quick pressure release. Serve hot.

Nutrition: Calories: 444kcal; Fat: 4g; Protein: 20g; Carbs: 82g

HERBY QUINOA WITH WALNUTS

Preparation time: 20 minutes **Cooking time:** 15 minutes **Servings:** 4

Ingredients:

- 2 minced sun-dried tomatoes
- 1 cup quinoa
- 2 cups vegetable broth
- 2 garlic cloves, minced
- ¼ cup chopped chives
- 2 tablespoons chopped parsley
- 2 tablespoons chopped basil
- 2 tablespoons chopped mint
- 1 tablespoon olive oil
- ½ teaspoon lemon zest
- 1 tablespoon lemon juice
- 2 tablespoons minced walnuts

Directions:

In a pot, combine quinoa, vegetable broth, and garlic. Boil until the quinoa is tender and the liquid absorbs for 10 to 15 minutes. Stir in chives, parsley, basil, mint, tomatoes, olive oil, zest, lemon juice, and walnuts. Warm for 5 minutes. Serve.

Nutrition: Calories: 308kcal; Fat: 8g; Protein: 28g; Carbs: 31g

CHIPOTLE KIDNEY BEAN CHILI

Preparation time: 20 minutes **Cooking time:** 25 minutes **Servings:** 4

Ingredients:

- 2 tablespoons olive oil
- 1 onion, chopped
- 2 garlic cloves, minced
- 1 (16-ounce 454-g) can tomato sauce
- 1 tablespoon chili powder
- 1 chipotle chili, minced
- 1 teaspoon ground cumin
- ½ teaspoon dried marjoram
- 1 can of kidney beans
- Sea salt and pepper to taste
- ½ teaspoon cayenne pepper

Directions:

Heat the oil in a pot over medium heat. Place in onion and garlic and sauté for 3 minutes. Put in tomato sauce, chipotle chili, chili powder, cumin, cayenne pepper, marjoram, salt, and pepper, and cook for 5 minutes. Stir in kidney beans and 2 cups of water. Bring to a boil, lower the heat and simmer for 15 minutes, stirring often.

Nutrition: Calories: 271kcal; Fat: 11g; Protein: 6g; Carbs: 37g

SOUTHERN BEAN BOWL

Preparation time: 15 minutes **Cooking time:** 0 minutes **Servings:** 4

Ingredients:

- 1 tomato, chopped
- 1 red bell pepper, chopped
- 1 green bell pepper, chopped
- 1 small red onion, sliced
- 1 (14½-ounce 411-g) can of black-eyed peas
- 1 (14½-ounce 411-g) can of black beans
- ¼ cup capers
- 2 avocados pitted
- 1 tablespoon lemon juice
- ¼ cup sake
- 1 teaspoon dried oregano
- Sea salt to taste
- 2 tablespoons olive oil
- 1 cup leafy greens, chopped

Directions:

Mix the tomato, peppers, onion, black-eyed peas, beans, and capers in a bowl. Put the avocados, lemon juice, sake, olive oil, oregano, and salt in a food processor and blitz until smooth. Add the dressing to the bean bowl and toss to combine. Top with leafy greens to serve.

Nutrition: Calories: 412kcal; Fat: 21g; Protein: 7g; Carbs: 48g

CREAM OF CORN SOUP

Preparation time: 5 minutes **Cooking time:**10 minutes **Servings:** 3
Ingredients:

- 2 tbsp. butter
- 2 tbsp. flour
- 1/8 tsp. black pepper
- 1 cup of water
- 1 cup liquid non-dairy creamer
- 2 jars (4.5 oz. non-dairy creamer) strained baby corn

Directions:
Thaw the butter in a saucepan, then add the black pepper and flour.
Stir well until smooth, then add the water and creamer. Mix well and
cook until the soup bubbles. Add the baby corn and mix well.
Serve.
Nutrition: Calories: 128Kcal; Protein: 0.6g; Carbohydrates: 8.1g;
Fat: 9.1g

CABBAGE BEEF BORSCHT

Preparation time: 5 minutes **Cooking time:** 2 hours **Servings:** 12
Ingredients:

- 2 tbsp. vegetable oil
- 3 lbs. beef short ribs
- 1/2 cup dry red wine
- 8 cups low-sodium chicken broth
- 1/2 tbs. berries
- 1/2 tbs. whole black peppercorns
- 1/2 tbs. coriander seeds
- 2 dill sprigs
- 2 oregano sprigs
- 2 parsley sprigs
- 2 tbsp. unsalted butter
- 3beets (1 1/2 lbs.), peeled and diced
- 1 small rutabaga (1/2 lb.), peeled and diced
- 1 leek, diced
- 1 small onion, diced (1 cup)
- 1/2 lb. carrots, diced
- 2 celery ribs, diced
- 1/2 head savoy cabbage (1 lb.), cored and shredded
- 7 oz. chopped tomatoes, canned
- 1/2 cup dry red wine
- 2 tbsp. red wine vinegar

- Freshly ground pepper
- 1/2 cup sour cream
- 1/4 cup chopped dill
- Horseradish, grated, for serving

Directions:
Start by placing the ribs in a large cooking pot and pour enough water to cover it.
Cover the beef pot and cook it on a simmer until it is tender, then shred it using a fork. Add the olive oil, rutabaga, carrots, shredded cabbage, and the remaining ingredients to the cooking liquid in the pot. Cover the cabbage soup and cook on low heat for 1 ½ hour. Serve warm.
Nutrition: Calories: 537Kcal; Protein: 18.7g; Carbohydrates: 10g; Fat: 45.5g

LEMON PEPPER BEEF SOUP

Preparation time: 5 minutes **Cooking time**: 35 minutes **Servings:** 6

Ingredients:

- 1 lb. lean ground beef
- 1/2 cup onion, chopped
- 2 tsp. lemon-pepper seasoning blend
- 1 cup beef broth
- 2 cups of water
- 1/3 cup white rice, uncooked
- 3 cups of frozen mixed vegetables
- 1 tbs. sour cream
- Cooking oil

Directions:

Spray a saucepan with cooking oil and place it over moderate heat. Toss in the onion and ground beef, and sauté until brown. Stir in the broth, and the rest of the ingredients, then boil. Reduce the heat to a simmer, then cover the soup to cook for another 30 minutes. Garnish with sour cream. Enjoy.

Nutrition: Calories: 252Kcal; Protein: 27.2g; Carbohydrates: 21.3g; Fat: 5.6g

CREAM OF CRAB SOUP

Preparation time: 5 minutes **Cooking time:** 20 minutes **Servings:** 4

Ingredients:

- 1 tbs. unsalted butter
- 1/2 medium onion, chopped
- 1/2 lb. imitation crab meat, shredded
- 1/4 low-sodium chicken broth
- 1 cup coffee creamer
- 2 tbsp. cornstarch
- 1/8 tsp. dillweed

Directions:
Add the butter to a cooking pan and melt it over moderate heat. Toss in the onion and sauté until soft, then stir in the crab meat. Stir-fry for 3 minutes then add the broth. Cook up to a boil, then reduce the heat to low. Whisk the coffee creamer with the cornstarch in a bowl until smooth. Place this cornstarch slurry to the soup and cook until it thickens. Stir in the dillweed and mix gently. Serve warm.
Nutrition: Calories: 232Kcal; Protein: 8.1g; Carbohydrates: 16.7g; Fat: 14.7g

CRAB AND SHRIMP GUMBO

Preparation time: 5 minutes **Cooking time:** 25 minutes **Servings:** 8

Ingredients:

- 1 cup bell pepper, chopped
- 1 1/2 cups onion, chopped
- 1 garlic clove, chopped
- 1/4 cup celery leaves, chopped
- 1 cup green onion tops
- 1/4 cup parsley, chopped
- 4 tbsp. olive oil
- 6 tbsp. flour
- 3 cups of water
- 4 cups chicken broth
- 8 oz. shrimp, uncooked
- 6 oz. crab meat
- 1/4 tsp. black pepper
- 1tsp. hot sauce
- 3 cups rice, cooked

Directions:

First, prepare the roux in a suitable pan by heating oil in it. Stir in the flour and sauté until it changes its color. Pour in 1 cup of water, then add the onion, garlic, celery leaves, and bell pepper. Cover the roux mixture and cook on low heat until the veggies turn soft. Add two more cups of water and the chicken broth, then mix again. Cook for 5 minutes, then add the crab meat and shrimp. Cook for 10 minutes, then add the parsley and green onion. Continue cooking for 5 minutes, then garnish with black pepper and hot sauce. Serve warm with rice.

Nutrition: Calories: 423Kcal; Protein: 17.8g; Carbohydrates: 47g; Fat: 9.2g

PEARL BARLEY AND RED BEANS SOUP

Preparation time: 8 minutes **Cooking time:** 25 minutes **Serving:** 6
Ingredients:

- 1 cup of Brussels sprouts
- 1 cup of boiled red kidney beans
- 1/2 cup cooked red lentils
- 5 cups low sodium vegetable broth
- 1 cup of pearl barley
- 1 tablespoon of thyme
- 1 tablespoon of turmeric
- 1 pinch of black pepper
- 1 pinch of salt

Directions:
Soak the Brussels sprouts in a bowl of cold water with a tablespoon of coarse salt for 10 minutes. After this time, remove the outer leaves and cut the shoots into quarters. Bring the vegetable broth to a boil and add the sprouts, beans, lentils, pearl barley, salt, and pepper. Cook over medium heat for about 25 minutes. Transfer to a mixer with the thyme and blend until puree is obtained.
Nutrition: calories: 129 / fat: 1 / protein: 7 / carbs: 20 /

SOUP OF MUSHROOMS AND TEMPEH

Preparation time: 5 minutes **Cooking time:** 25 minutes **Service:** 3
Ingredients:

- 1 lb of cremini mushrooms
- 1/2 cup of tempeh
- 2 yellow onions
- 5 cups low sodium vegetable broth
- 3 tablespoons of rice flour
- 1 tablespoon of parsley
- 1 pinch of black pepper
- 1 pinch of salt
- 2 tablespoons of olive oil

Directions:
Clean the mushrooms and cut them. Put the olive oil in a saucepan with the chopped onions and parsley and brown them for 5 minutes. Add the vegetable broth and the diced tempeh and cook for about 25 minutes. Add the rice flour and mix for 5 minutes. Transfer all the ingredients to a mixer and blend until creamy.
Nutrition: calories: 206 / fat: 13 / protein: 13 / carbs: 15 /

CAULIFLOWER AND MISO SOUP

Preparation time: 5 minutes **Cooking time:** 30 minutes **Serving:** 3
Ingredients:

- 1 cauliflower
- 1 tablespoon of Miso
- 2 yellow onions
- 2 carrots
- 5 cups low sodium vegetable broth
- 1 tablespoon of parsley
- 1 pinch of black pepper
- 1 pinch of salt
- 2 tablespoons of coconut oil

Directions:
In a saucepan, sauté the chopped onions for 5 minutes, add the chopped cabbage and the chopped carrots, and cook for 5 minutes, stirring with a cooking spoon. Add the vegetable stock, salt, pepper, and parsley. Cook over moderate heat for about 25 minutes, add the miso and cook for another minute. Transfer all the ingredients to a mixer and blend until creamy.
Nutrition: calories: 183 / fat: 4 / protein: 9 / carbs: 33 /

ASPARAGUS AND TAMARI SOUP

Preparation time: 5 minutes **Cooking time:** 25 minutes **Service:** 2

Ingredients:

- 2 sweet potatoes
- 1 cup of asparagus
- 2 tablespoons of Tamari
- 3 cups low sodium vegetable broth
- 1 cup of coconut water
- 1 tablespoon of basil
- 1 pinch of black pepper
- 1 pinch of salt
- 1 tablespoon of olive oil

Directions:
Peel and cut the potatoes into cubes, clean the asparagus, and cut them into small pieces. Put the vegetable broth and coconut water in a saucepan, bring to a boil and add the potatoes, asparagus, salt, pepper, olive oil, and basil and cook over medium heat for about 25 minutes. Transfer to the food processor and blend until creamy. Season with the tamari and serve hot.

Nutrition: calories: 228 / fat: 8 / protein: 6 / carbs: 37 /

OVEN BEEF STEW

Preparation time: 15 minute **Cooking time:** 4 hours **Servings:** 8
Ingredients:

- 1 lb beef stew meat, cut into 1-inch cubes
- 2 cups of cubed potatoes
- 2 cups of chopped carrots
- 1 can of condensed cream of mushroom soup
- 1 can of condensed French onion soup
- 1 ¾ cup of water
- 1 cups of frozen green peas

Directions:
In a 2- to 3-quart casserole dish, combine the stew meat, potatoes, carrots, mushroom soup, French onion soup, and water. Completely combine. Bake uncovered for 4 to 5 hours, stirring once or twice. Add the peas 15 minutes before serving.
Nutrition: 618 cals; protein 41g; carbs 33.7g; fat 42.9g; sodium 544.2mg.

HARVEST BEEF STEW

Preparation time: 30 minute **Cooking time**: 1 hr 30 minute
Servings: 6
Ingredients:

- 4 tbsp. bacon drippings
- ¼ cups of flour
- Salt and pepper to taste
- 2 ½ lbs beef stew meat, cut into 1 inch cubes
- 5 tbsp. olive oil
- 1 onion, thinly sliced
- 6 cloves garlic, thinly sliced
- 1 lb carrots, peeled and sliced
- 1 lb celery, sliced
- ¼ cup of rice vinegar
- 2 tbsp. brown sugar
- 4 cups of beef broth
- 2 (12 fluid Oz.) cans or bottles of ale
- 1 parsnip, peeled and sliced
- 1 turnip, peeled and chopped
- 1 lb baby red potatoes, washed
- ¾ cup of parsley, chopped
- 4 whole bay leaves

Directions:
Warm the bacon fat in a large pot over medium heat.Combine the
flour, salt, and pepper. Cover the beef cubes with foil. Brown the

102

meat finely in the bacon fat. Remove it and place it on a paper towel. Warm the olive oil in the same pot. Sauté celery, carrots, onions, and garlic over low heat. The vinegar and sugar. After adding the broth, bring to a boil. The pan can be deglazed by removing the accumulated food on its bottom. Pour the beer into the pot, then add the red potatoes, parsley, bay leaves, and parsnips. Turn the heat down to medium-low. 90 minutes of covered simmering with occasional stirring.

Nutrition: 918 cals; protein 56g; carbs 43.7g; fat 52.9g; chole 166.3mg; sodium 777.2mg.

BEEF AND VEGETABLE STEW

Preparation time: 15 minute **Cooking time:** 2 hours 15 minutes
Servings: 6
Ingredients:

- 1 tbsp. vegetable oil
- 1 lb cubed beef stew meat, trimmed
- 1 onion, thinly sliced
- 1 (6 Oz.) can of tomato paste
- 1 (14.5 Oz.) can low fat, low sodium beef broth
- 3 potatoes, cubed
- 1 cup of chopped carrots
- 1 tsp. Dried thyme
- ¼ tsp. crushed red pepper flakes
- 1 sprig of fresh rosemary
- 1 bay leaf
- 10 Oz. button mushrooms, quartered

- 1 package of frozen green peas, thawed

Directions:
Oil in a big pot is heated up over medium-high heat. About 10 minutes after adding the beef, brown all sides of the meat before removing and setting aside. In the same saucepan, combine tomato paste and onion; heat and stir for about 5 minutes, or until the onion are soft. Add beef broth and add the beef back to the pot. Reduce heat to low, cover, and simmer for 1 to 1 1/2 hours or until meat is tender. Add the potatoes, carrots, rosemary, crushed red pepper flakes, and bay leaf. Cover the saucepan and simmer for 45 minutes. If the stew becomes too thick, add a little water. Add the mushrooms and peas; simmer and stir for 10 to 15 minutes, or until heated. Before serving, take off the bay leaf and rosemary sprig.
Nutrition: 367 cals; protein 31.1g; carbs 36.9g; fat 11.1g; sodium 369.8mg.

SEsAME Couscous CHIcKEN

Preparation time: 10 minutes **Cooking time**: 18 minutes **Serves:** 3
Ingredients:

- Water,
- 1-1/2 cups Whole-wheat couscous,
- 1 cup Olive oil,
- 1-2 tablespoons Coleslaw mix,
- 2.5 cups Diced green onions,
- 4 Sesame salad dressing,
- 2-3 tablespoons Baked chicken breast,
- 2.5 cups Chopped cilantro,

Direction:
Bring 1-1/2 cups of water to a simmer inside a small saucepan. Mix in the couscous. Now remove from heat, then let it stand, covered, for 6-11 minutes, or until the water has been absorbed. Fluff using a fork. Warm the oil inside a large nonstick pan over a medium flame. Include coleslaw mixture; bake while stirring for 5-6 minutes or when the coleslaw mixture becomes tender. Then add diced green onions, 2.5 tablespoons of sesame salad dressing, and couscous and cook for some time. Transfer couscous from skillet to a table; keep warm. Bake and stir the chicken and leftover dressing in the same pan over medium flame until heated. If desired, end up serving over couscous and garnish with cilantro and chopped peanuts.
Nutrition: calories 9g, Net Carbs: 35g, Protein: 26g, Sodium: 442mg

FIRE-ROASTED TOMATOES OVER CHICKEN

Preparation time: 10 minutes **Cooking time:** 20 minutes **Serving:** 2
Ingredients:

- Garlic-herb blend,
- 2.5 tablespoons Salt,
- 1/2 teaspoon Italian seasoning,
- 1-1/4 teaspoon Pepper,
- 1/4 teaspoon red pepper flakes,
- 1/8 teaspoon (optional) Debone chicken breast,
- 4 Olive oil,
- 1-2 tablespoons Chopped tomatoes,
- 1 can Chopped green beans,
- 3/4-pound water,
- 2 tablespoons Butter,
- 1 tablespoon cooked pasta, optional

Instructions.
Combine the seasoning ingredients and sprinkle on the chicken breasts' sides. Warm the oil inside a big pan on a medium flame. Brown all sides of the chicken. Add chopped tomatoes and bring to a simmer. Reduce heat to low and cover for 11-13 minutes, otherwise, until a digital thermometer inserted into the chicken reaches 165°. Meanwhile, mix green beans and tomatoes with water inside a 2-quart oven-safe dish; microwave at high temperature for 5-6 minutes until tender. Drain. Now remove the chicken from the pan; keep warm. Whisk in the butter and chopped beans into the prepared tomato mixture. End up serving with chicken and cooked pasta, if needed.

Nutrition: Fat: 10g, Net Carbs: 12g, Protein: 37g, Sodium: 681mg

BUNLESS SLOPPY JOES

Preparation time: 15 minutes **Cooking time:** 40 minutes **Serves** 6
Ingredients:

- 6 small sweet potatoes
- 1 pound lean ground beef
- 1 onion, finely chopped
- 1 carrot, finely chopped
- ¼ cup finely chopped mushrooms
- ¼ cup finely chopped red bell pepper
- 3 garlic cloves, minced
- 2 teaspoons Worcestershire sauce
- 1 tablespoon white wine vinegar
- 1 (15-ounce / 425-g) can low-sodium tomato sauce
- 2 tablespoons tomato paste

Direction:

Preheat the oven to 400 ℉ . In a baking dish, arrange the sweet potatoes in a single layer. Cook for 25 to 40 minutes, depending on size, or until soft and cooked. While the sweet potatoes are baking, brown the beef in a large skillet over medium heat, breaking it up into small pieces as you stir. Sauté the onion, carrot, mushrooms, bell pepper, and garlic for 1 minute. Combine the Worcestershire sauce, vinegar, tomato sauce, and paste in a mixing bowl. Bring to a simmer, then reduce to low heat for 5 minutes to allow the flavors to meld. Serve 1/2 cup of the meat mixture on each baked potato.

Nutrition: calories: 372 | fat: 19g | protein: 16g | carbs: 34g | sugars: 13g | fiber: 6g | sodium: 161mg

BEEF CURRY

Preparation time: 15 minutes **Cooking time:** 10 minutes **Serves** 6
Ingredients:

- 1 tablespoon extra-virgin olive oil
- 1 small onion, thinly sliced
- 2 teaspoons minced fresh ginger
- 3 garlic cloves, minced
- 2 teaspoons ground coriander
- 1 teaspoon ground cumin
- 1 jalapeño or serrano pepper, slit lengthwise but not all the way through
- ¼ teaspoon ground turmeric
- ¼ teaspoon salt
- 1 pound grass-fed sirloin tip steak, top round steak, or top sirloin steak, cut into bite-size pieces
- 2 tablespoons chopped fresh cilantro

Direction:
Heat the oil in a large skillet over medium-high heat. Cook for 3 to 5 minutes until the onion is caramelized and softened. Stir in the ginger and garlic for about 30 seconds, or until fragrant. Combine the coriander, cumin, jalapeno, turmeric, and salt in a small bowl. Stir continually for 1 minute after adding the spice combination to the skillet. With roughly a quarter cup of water, deglaze the skillet. Stir in the meat for approximately 5 minutes, or until well-browned but still medium-rare. Take out the jalapeno. Serve with cilantro on top.
Nutrition:calories: 140 | fat: 7g | protein: 18g | carbs: 3g | sugars: 1g | fiber: 1g | sodium: 141mg

ASIAN GRILLED BEEF SALAD

Preparation time: 15 minutes **Cooking time:** 15 minutes **Serves** 4
Ingredients:

- ¼ cup freshly squeezed lime juice
- 1 tablespoon low-sodium tamari or gluten-free soy sauce
- 1 tablespoon extra-virgin olive oil
- 1 garlic clove, minced
- 1 teaspoon honey
- ¼ teaspoon red pepper flakes Salad:
- 1 pound grass-fed flank steak
- ¼ teaspoon salt
- Pinch ground black pepper
- 6 cups chopped leaf lettuce
- 1 cucumber, halved lengthwise and thinly cut into half moons
- ½ small red onion, sliced
- 1 carrot, cut into ribbons
- ¼ cup chopped fresh cilantro

Direction:

Prepare your ingredients. Whisk the lime juice, tamari, olive oil, garlic, honey, and red pepper flakes in a small bowl. Place aside. Assemble the Salad Season on both sides of the steak with salt and pepper. Heat a skillet over high heat until it is smoking hot. Cook the beef for 3 to 6 minutes per side, depending on how well done you want it. Tent with aluminum foil and set aside for 10 minutes. In a large mixing bowl, combine the lettuce, cucumber, onion, carrot, and cilantro. Place the steak in the salad dish after thinly slicing it against the grain. Mix the dressing into the salad. Serve.

Nutrition: calories: 231 | fat: 10g | protein: 26g | carbs: 10g | sugars: 4g | fiber: 2g | sodium: 349m

MUSTARD GLAZED PORK CHOPS

Preparation time: 5 minutes **Cooking time:** 25 minutes **Serves** 4
Ingredients:

- ¼ cup Dijon mustard
- 1 tablespoon pure maple syrup
- 2 tablespoons rice vinegar
- 4 bone-in, thin-cut pork chops

Instructions:
Preheat the oven to 400°F. Combine the mustard, maple syrup, and rice vinegar in a small saucepan. Stir to mix and bring to a simmer over medium heat. Cook for about 2 minutes until just slightly thickened. In a baking dish, place the pork chops and spoon the sauce over them, flipping to coat. Bake for 20 to 22 minutes until the juices run clear.
Nutrition: calories: 257 | fat: 7g | protein: 39g | carbs: 7g | sugars: 4g | fiber: 0g | sodium: 466mg

PARMESAN-CRUSTED PORK CHOPS

Preparation time: 10 minutes **Cooking time:** 25 minutes **Serves** 4
Ingredients:

- Nonstick cooking spray
- 4 bone-in, thin-cut pork chops
- 2 tablespoons butter
- ½ cup grated Parmesan cheese
- 3 garlic cloves, minced
- ¼ teaspoon salt
- ¼ teaspoon dried thyme
- Freshly ground black pepper, to taste

Direction:

Preheat the oven to 400 ℉ . Spray a baking sheet with nonstick cooking spray and line with parchment paper. Arrange the pork chops on the prepared baking sheet, ensuring they don't overlap. Mix butter, cheese, garlic, salt, thyme, and pepper in a small bowl. Top each pork chop with 2 tablespoons of the cheese mixture. Bake for 18 to 22 minutes until the pork is thoroughly cooked and the juices run clear. Preheat the broiler to high and brown the tops for 1 to 2 minutes.

Nutrition: Calories: 332 | fat: 16g | protein: 44g | carbs: 1g | sugars: 0g | fiber: 0g | sodium: 440mg

CHERRY-GLAZED LAMB CHOPS

Preparation time: 10 minutes **Cooking time:** 20 minutes **Serves** 4
Ingredients:

- 4 (4-ounce / 113-g) lamb chops
- 1½ teaspoons chopped fresh rosemary
- ¼ teaspoon salt
- ¼ teaspoon freshly ground black pepper
- 1 cup frozen cherries, thawed
- ¼ cup dry red wine
- 2 tablespoons orange juice
- 1 teaspoon extra-virgin olive oil Season the lamb chops with rosemary, salt, and pepper.

Direction:
Combine the cherries, red wine, and orange juice in a small saucepan over medium-low heat and cook, occasionally stirring, until the sauce thickens, about 8 to 10 minutes. Over medium-high heat, heat a large skillet. Drizzle in enough olive oil to coat the bottom lightly when the pan is hot. Cook the lamb chops on each side for 3 to 4 minutes, or until medium-rare. Serve with a cherry glaze on top.

Nutrition: calories: 356 | fat: 27g | protein: 20g | carbs: 6g | sugars: 4g | fiber: 1g | sodium: 199mg

LAMB AND VEGETABLE STEW

Preparation time: 10 minutes **Cooking time:** 3 to 6 hours **Serves** 6
Ingredients:

- 1 pound boneless lamb stew meat
- 1-pound turnips, peeled and chopped
- 1 fennel bulb, trimmed and thinly sliced
- 10 ounces mushrooms, sliced
- 1 onion, diced
- 3 garlic cloves, minced
- 2 cups low-sodium chicken broth
- 2 tablespoons tomato paste
- ¼ cup dry red wine (optional)
- 1 teaspoon chopped fresh thyme
- ½ teaspoon salt
- ¼ teaspoon freshly ground black pepper
- Chopped fresh parsley for garnish

Instructions:
Combine the lamb, turnips, fennel, mushrooms, onion, garlic, chicken broth, tomato paste, red wine (if using), thyme, salt, and pepper in a slow cooker. Cook on high for 3 hours or low for 6 hours, covered. Garnish with parsley and serve when the meat is tender and falling apart. If you don't have a slow cooker, sear the lamb on all sides in a large pot with two teaspoons of olive oil over medium heat. Set aside after removing from the pot. Cook the turnips, fennel, mushrooms, onion, and garlic for 3 to 4 minutes, or until the vegetables soften. Combine the chicken broth, tomato paste, red wine (if using), thyme, salt, pepper, and browned lamb in a mixing

bowl. Bring to a boil, then reduce to low heat. Cook for 1 1/2 to 2 hours, or until the meat is tender. Serve garnished with parsley.

Nutrition: calories: 303 | fat: 7g | protein: 32g | carbs: 27g | sugars: 7g | fiber: 4g | sodium: 310mg

LEMON-PEPPER TILAPIA

Preparation time: 5 minutes **Cooking time:** 15 minutes **Serving:** 6

Ingredients:

- 6 Tilapia fillets,

- 2 tablespoons Butter,

- 2 teaspoons Grated lemon zest,1 tablespoon Lemon juice,
- 1 teaspoon Garlic salt,

- 1 teaspoon Paprika,

- 1/2 teaspoon Black pepper,

- 1/4 cup Fresh parsley

Direction:

Preheat the oven to 430 °F. In a 15x10x1-inch baking dish, place the fish. Then, melt the butter in a microwave-safe bowl and stir in the lemon zest and juice. Next, Season the fish with salt, garlic, and black pepper and drizzle with the melted butter. Finally, bake in the oven for 10-12 minutes or until the fish flakes easily with a fork. Enjoy with a parsley garnish.

Nutrition: Fat: 5g, Net Carbs: 2g, Protein: 32g, Sodium: 254mg

ROSEMARY LAMB CHOPS

Preparation time: 25 minutes **Cooking time:** 10 minutes **Serves** 4
Ingredients:

- 1½ pounds lamb chops (4 small chops)
- 1 teaspoon kosher salt Leaves from
- 1 (6-inch) rosemary sprig
- 2 tablespoons avocado oil
- 1 shallot, peeled and cut in quarters
- 1 tablespoon tomato paste
- 1 cup beef broth

Instructions:

On a chopping board, place the lamb chops. Salt and rosemary leaves should be pressed into both sides of the chops. Allow for 15 to 30 minutes of resting time at room temperature. Select Sauté/More on the electric pressure cooker. Add the avocado oil once the pan is heated. 2 minutes per side to brown the lamb chops (Brown them in batches if they don't all fit in one layer.) Place the chops on a serving plate. Combine the shallot, tomato paste, and broth in a pot. Cook for approximately a minute, scraping up the brown pieces from the bottom. Select Cancel. Return the chops to the pot, along with any accumulated juices. Close and lock the pressure cooker's lid. Set the valve to the closed position. Cook for 2 minutes on high pressure. When the cooking is finished, press Cancel and release the tension quickly. Unlock and remove the cover once the pin has dropped. Place the lamb chops on plates right away and serve.

Nutrition: calories: 233 | fat: 18g | protein: 15g | carbs: 1g | sugars: 1g | fiber: 0g | sodium: 450mg

ROASTED PORK LOIN

Preparation time: 5 minutes **Cooking time:** 40 minutes **Serves** 4
Ingredients:

- 1 pound pork loin
- 1 tablespoon extra-virgin olive oil, divided
- 2 teaspoons honey
- ¼ teaspoon freshly ground black pepper
- ½ teaspoon dried rosemary
- 2 small gold potatoes, chopped into 2-inch cubes
- 4 (6-inch) carrots, chopped into
- ½-inch rounds

Instructions:
Preheat the oven to 350° F. 12 tbsp of oil and honey are rubbed into the pork loin. Season with rosemary and pepper. Toss the potatoes and carrots in the remaining 1/2 tbsp of oil in a medium bowl. Place the pork and vegetables in a single layer on a baking pan. The cooking time is 40 minutes. Before slicing, remove the baking sheet from the oven and allow the pork to rest for at least 10 minutes. Make four equal pieces of pork and vegetables.
Nutrition: Calories: 343 | fat: 10g | protein: 26g | carbs: 26g | sugars: 6g | fiber: 4g | sodium: 109mg

CHICKEN CHILI

Preparation Time: 6 minutes **Cooking Time:** 1 hour **Serves:** 4
Ingredients:

- 3 tablespoons vegetable oil
- 2 cloves garlic, minced
- 1 green bell pepper, chopped
- 1 onion, chopped
- 1 stalk celery, sliced
- 1/4-pound mushrooms, chopped
- 1-pound chicken breast
- 1 tablespoon chili powder
- 1 teaspoon dried oregano
- 1 teaspoon ground cumin
- 1/2 teaspoon paprika
- 1/2 teaspoon cocoa powder
- 1/4 teaspoon salt
- 1 pinch of crushed red pepper flakes
- 1 pinch of ground black pepper
- 1 (14.5 oz) can of tomatoes with juice
- 1 (19 oz) can of kidney beans

Direction:
Fill 2 tablespoons of oil into a big skillet and heat it moderately. Add mushrooms, celery, onion, bell pepper, and garlic, and sauté for 5 minutes. Put it to one side. Insert the leftover 1 tablespoon of oil into the skillet. Cook the chicken until browned and its exterior turns firm at high heat. Transfer the vegetable mixture back into the skillet. Stir in ground black pepper, hot pepper flakes, salt, cocoa powder,

paprika, oregano, cumin, and chili powder. Continue stirring for several minutes to avoid burning. Pour the beans and tomatoes, lead the mixture to the boiling point, and adjust the setting to low heat. Place a lid on the skillet and leave it simmering for 15 minutes. Uncover the skillet and leave it simmering for another 15 minutes.
Nutrition: 308 Calories; 25.9g Carbohydrate; 29g Protein

CHICKEN VERA CRUZ

Preparation Time: 7 minutes **Cooking Time:** 10 hours **Serves:** 5
Ingredients:

- 1 medium onion, cut into wedges
- 1-pound yellow-skin potatoes
- 6 skinless, boneless chicken thighs
- 2 (14.5 oz.) cans of no-salt-added diced tomatoes
- 1 fresh jalapeño chili pepper
- 2 tablespoons Worcestershire sauce
- 1 tablespoon chopped garlic
- 1 teaspoon dried oregano, crushed
- ¼ teaspoon ground cinnamon
- 1/8 teaspoon ground cloves
- ½ cup snipped fresh parsley
- ¼ cup chopped pimiento-stuffed green olives

Direction:
Put the onion in a 3 1/2- or 4-quart slow cooker. Place chicken thighs and potatoes on top. Drain and discard juices from a can of tomatoes. Stir undrained and drained tomatoes, cloves, cinnamon, oregano, garlic, Worcestershire sauce, and jalapeño pepper together in a bowl. Pour over all in the cooker. Cook with a cover for 10 hours in a low-heat setting. Stir chopped pimiento-stuffed green olives and snip fresh parsley together in a small bowl to make the topping. Drizzle the topping over each serving of chicken.
Nutrition: 228 Calories; 9g Sugar; 25g Carbohydrate

CHICKEN AND CORNMEAL DUMPLINGS

Preparation Time: 8 minutes **Cooking Time:** 8 hours **Serves:** 4
Ingredients:

- Chicken and Vegetable Filling
- 2 medium carrots, thinly sliced
- 1 stalk celery, thinly sliced
- 1/3 cup corn kernels
- ½ of a medium onion, thinly sliced
- 2 cloves garlic, minced
- 1 teaspoon snipped fresh rosemary
- ¼ teaspoon ground black pepper
- 2 chicken thighs, skinned
- 1 cup reduced-sodium chicken broth
- ½ cup fat-free milk
- 1 tablespoon all-purpose flour Cornmeal Dumplings
- ¼ cup flour
- ¼ cup cornmeal
- ½ teaspoon baking powder
- 1 egg white
- 1 tablespoon fat-free milk
- 1 tablespoon canola oil

Direction:
Mix 1/4 teaspoon pepper, carrots, garlic, celery, rosemary, corn, and onion in a 1 1/2 or 2-quart slow cooker. Place chicken on top. Pour the broth atop the mixture into the cooker. Close and cook on low heat for 7 to 8 hours. If cooking with the low-heat setting, switch to a

high-heat setting (or if the heat setting is unavailable, continue to cook). Place the chicken onto a cutting board and let it cool slightly. Once cool enough to handle, chop off the chicken bones and get rid of them bones. Chop the chicken and place it back into the mixture in the cooker. Mix flour and milk in a small bowl until smooth. Stir into the mix in the range. Drop the Cornmeal Dumplings dough into 4 mounds atop the hot chicken mixture using two spoons. Cover and cook for 20 to 25 minutes or until a toothpick comes out clean when inserted into a dumpling. (Avoid lifting the lid when cooking.) Sprinkle each of the servings with coarse pepper if desired. Mix 1/2 teaspoon baking powder, 1/4 cup flour, a dash of salt, and 1/4 cup cornmeal in a medium bowl. Mix 1 tablespoon canola oil, 1 egg white, and 1 tablespoon fat-free milk in a small bowl. Pour the egg mixture into the flour mixture. Mix just until moistened.
Nutrition: 369 Calories; 9g Sugar; 47g Carbohydrate

GAZPACHO

Preparation Time: 15 minutes **Cooking Time:** 0 minutes **Serves** 4
Ingredients:

- 3 pounds of ripe tomatoes
- 1 cup low-sodium tomato juice
- ½ red onion, chopped
- 1 cucumber
- 1 red bell pepper
- 2 celery stalks
- 2 tablespoons parsley
- 2 garlic cloves
- 2 tablespoons extra-virgin olive oil
- 2 tablespoons red wine vinegar
- 1 teaspoon honey
- ½ teaspoon salt
- ¼ teaspoon freshly ground black pepper

Direction:
Combine the tomatoes, tomato juice, onion, cucumber, bell pepper,
celery, parsley, garlic, olive oil, vinegar, honey, salt, and pepper in a
blender jar. Pulse until blended but still slightly chunky. Adjust the
seasonings as needed and serve.
Nutrition: 170 Calories; 24g Carbohydrates; 16g Sugars

TOMATO AND KALE SOUP

Preparation Time: 10 minutes **Cooking Time:** 15 minutes **Serves:** 4

Ingredients:

- 1 tablespoon extra-virgin olive oil
- 1 medium onion
- 2 carrots
- 3 garlic cloves
- 4 cups low-sodium vegetable broth
- 1 (28-ounce) can of crushed tomatoes
- ½ teaspoon dried oregano
- ¼ teaspoon dried basil
- 4 cups chopped baby kale leaves
- ¼ teaspoon salt

Direction:

In a huge pot, heat oil over medium heat. Sauté onion and carrots for 3 to 5 minutes. Add the garlic and sauté for 30 seconds more until fragrant. Add the vegetable broth, tomatoes, oregano, and basil to the pot and boil. Decrease the heat to low and simmer for 5 minutes. Using an immersion blender, purée the soup. Add the kale and simmer for three more minutes. Season with salt. Serve immediately.

Nutrition facts: 170 Calories; 31g Carbohydrates; 13g Sugars

SQUASH SOUP WITH CRISPY CHICKPEAS

Preparation Time: 10 minutes **Cooking Time:** 20 minutes **Serves:** 4

Ingredients:

- 1 (15-ounce) can of low-sodium chickpeas
- 1 teaspoon extra-virgin olive oil
- ¼ teaspoon smoked paprika
- Pinch salt, plus ½ teaspoon
- 3 medium zucchinis
- 3 cups low-sodium vegetable broth
- ½ onion
- 3 garlic cloves
- 2 tablespoons plain low-fat Greek yogurt
- Freshly ground black pepper

Direction:
Preheat the oven to 425°F. Line a baking sheet with parchment paper. In a medium mixing bowl, toss the chickpeas with 1 teaspoon of olive oil, the smoked paprika, and a pinch of salt. Transfer to the prepared baking sheet and roast until crispy, about 20 minutes, stirring once. Set aside. Meanwhile, heat the remaining 1 tablespoon of oil in a medium pot over medium heat. Add the zucchini, broth, onion, and garlic to the pot, and boil. Simmer, and cook for 20 minutes. In a blender jar, purée the soup. Return to the pot. Add the yogurt and remaining ½ teaspoon salt and pepper and stir well. Serve topped with roasted chickpeas.
Nutrition: 188 Calories; 24g Carbohydrates; 7g Sugars

VEGETARIAN CHILI

Preparation time: 15 minutes **Cooking time:** 360 minutes **Serving:** 6

Ingredients:

- Chopped tomatoes,
- 28.5-ounces Vegetable broth,
- 4-5 cups Black beans,
- 15.5-ounces Cannellini beans,
- 15.5-ounces red kidney beans,
- 15.5-ounces Frozen lima beans,
- 1-1/2 cups Diced onion,
- 1 cup green bell pepper, diced and seeded,
- 1 Chopped garlic clove,
- 2 Pickled jalapenos,
- 1 tablespoon Chili powder,
- 2.5 tablespoons oregano,
- 2 tablespoons Ground cumin,
- 2.5 teaspoons Ground coriander,
- 1.5 teaspoons Hot sauce,
- 1.5 teaspoons couscous,
- 1/3 cup Jack cheese, shredded,
- 1-1/2 cups Diced cilantro,
- 1/3 cup Salt, to taste
- Black pepper, to taste

Direction:

Combine all ingredients, couscous, jack cheese, diced cilantro, and salt inside a slow cooker. Cover and cook the ingredients on high flame for 3-4 hours. Include couscous 5-10 minutes before serving. Cook, covered until couscous is soft. Sprinkle with salt and black pepper. Garnish each serving with jack cheese as well as cilantro. Enjoy!

Nutrition: Fat: 3g, Net Carbs: 7g, Protein: 5g, Sodium: 198mg

ITALIAN STYLE EGGPLANT CASSEROLE

Preparation time: 10 minutes **Cooking time:** 50 minutes **Serving:** 4

Ingredients:

- Eggplant, cut into cubes,
- 1 whole-wheat breadcrumb,
- 1.5 cups Egg substitute,
- 1 cup Garlic powder,
- 1-1/2 teaspoons Italian seasoning,
- 1-1/4 teaspoon Pepper,
- 1/8 teaspoon Salt,
- 1/8 Diced tomatoes,

Direction:
Bring 3-inches of water to a simmer inside a soup pot on low flame. Include eggplant and cook for about 22-32 minutes, until the eggplant is soft; drain any liquid. Preheat the oven to 350°Fahrenheit. Coat a 10-inch square baking tray using cooking spray. Mash the eggplant using a spoon inside a medium bowl. Whisk in 1/2 cup bread crumbs, egg substitute, then Italian seasoning, with garlic, salt, and black pepper. Layout the eggplant mixture within the prepared baking tray, then top with tomato pieces. Garnish the tomatoes with the leftover bread crumbs, then cook the spray. Cook for 25-30 minutes until the tomatoes are soft and browned around the edges. Serve hot.
Nutrition: Fat: 1g, Net Carbs: 14g, Protein: 6g, Sodium: 181mg

VEGGIE-STUFFED BURRITOS

Preparation time: 10 minutes **Cooking time:** 25 minutes **Serving:** 4

Ingredients:

- Vegetable oil,
- 1.5 teaspoon Diced onions,
- 2 Chopped garlic cloves,
- 3 Green bell pepper, diced,
- 1 Diced zucchini,
- 1 Grated carrot,
- 1 Chili powder,
- 2.5 teaspoons Dried oregano,
- 1.5 teaspoons Ground cumin,
- 1.5 teaspoons Salsa,
- 1 cup Black beans, soak-drain,
- 16.5-ounce Flour tortillas,
- 5 Cheddar cheese, half-skim, 1/2 cup

Direction:

Preheat your oven to 400°F. Cover a 9-by-13-inch baking tray with cooking spray. Warm the oil inside a large pan over medium flame; include the onion, then bake for 4 minutes, or until soft, while stirring occasionally. Include the garlic, followed by green pepper, and zucchini, including carrot, then bake for 6 minutes while stirring often. Whisk in the chili powder and oregano, then cumin, and mix well. Remove the pan from the flame and whisk in 1/4 cup salsa with beans. Spoon equivalent proportions of the veggie mixture into the middle of the tortillas. Now fold the lower end of every tortilla over the veggie mixture, then fold all sides to make an envelope shape.

Fold over the tops of every tortilla to close; put seam side down within the baking tray. Distribute the remaining salsa equally over the burritos. Cook for 16 minutes. Garnish with the cheddar cheese, then cook for 6 minutes, unless the cheese melts. Serve right away.
Nutrition: Fat: 7g, Net Carbs: 25g, Protein: 19g, Sodium: 846mg

ARTICHOKE QUICHE

Preparation time: 15 minutes **Cooking time:** 70 minutes **Serving:** 6

Ingredients:

- Cooked long-grain rice,
- 2.5 cups Cheddar cheese, half-skim,
- 3/2 cup Egg substitute,
- 3/2 cup Dried dill weed,
- 1.5 teaspoons Salt,
- 1/2 teaspoon Smashed garlic clove,
- 1 Cooking spray
- Artichoke hearts, cubed,
- 14.5-ounces Skimmed milk,
- 3/4 cup green onions, diced,
- 1/4 cup Dijon mustard,
- 1.5 tablespoons Ground white pepper,
- 1-1/4 teaspoon Green onion flakes

Direction:
Preheat the oven to 350°Fahrenheit. Combine the rice, 1/2 cup cheese, and 1/2 cup egg substitute, followed by dillweed, salt, and garlic; press a 10-inch pie-plate coated using cooking spray. Cook for 6 minutes at 350°Fahrenheit. Organize artichoke on the bottom of the rice crust; scatter with the remaining cheddar cheese equally. Combine the rest of the egg substitute and some milk, followed by 3 ingredients; garnish on cheese. Preheat the oven to 350°Fahrenheit and cook for 55-minutes, or until set. Allow cooling for 5 minutes; slice in wedges. Scatter with green onion flakes, If desired. Serve and enjoy!

Nutrition: Fat: 2g, Net Carbs: 23g, Protein: 10g, Sodium: 490mg

BLUE CHEESE FIELD SALAD

Preparation time: 5 minutes **Cooking time:** 0 minutes **Serving:** 2
Ingredients:

- Salad greens,
- 5 ounces Chopped red pear,
- 1 Blue cheese,
- 1-1/4 cup Raspberry vinaigrette,
- 3 tablespoons Walnuts, thinly diced,

direction:
Inside a big mixing bowl, combine the first three items. Add dressing, then gently toss. Now spoon within plates as well as garnish evenly with walnuts.
Nutrition: Fat: 5g, Net Carbs: 11g, Protein: 3g, Sodium: 140mg

SPICY ASPARAGUS-TEMPEH

Preparation time: 12 minutes **Cooking time:** 10 minutes **Serving:** 4

Ingredients:

- Asparagus spears,
- 3/2-pound Vegetable broth,
- 3/2 cup Soy sauce,
- 1/3 cup Cornstarch,
- 2 teaspoons Sesame oil,
- 2.5 tablespoons Multigrain tempeh,
- 8.5-ounces Chopped garlic cloves,
- 4 Crushed red pepper,
- 1 teaspoon Shiitake mushrooms,
- 6.5-ounces Cooked brown rice,

Direction:
Remove the tough ends of the asparagus spears. Cut each spear into 2-inch slices diagonally. Place aside. Combine the following three ingredients inside a small bowl unless smooth. Place aside in a big nonstick pan over a moderate flame, warm 1 tablespoon oil. Include tempeh and stir-fry for 5 to 6 minutes, or until lightly golden. Remove the tempeh from the pan and put it aside. Inside the same pan, heat the remaining oil. Include garlic, and red pepper, followed by asparagus spears and mushrooms, then stir-fry for 4 minutes or until the asparagus is tender. Include the prepared broth mixture, and simmer for 3 to 4 minutes or until the sauce thickens. Add tempeh, then cook for 1 minute more, or until the tempeh is done. End up serving over brown rice. Enjoy!

Nutrition Facts Fat: 14g, Net Carbs: 49g, Protein: 18g, Sodium: 745mg

VEGGIE CHEDDAR FRITTATA

Preparation time: 5 minutes **Cooking time:** 12 minutes **Serving:** 4
Ingredients:

- Cooking spray
- Green bell pepper,
- 1 pre-diced mushroom,
- 8 ounces of Vegetable sausage,
- 1 ounce Salt,
- 1/8 teaspoon Pepper,
- 1/8 teaspoon Egg substitute,
- 1/2 cup Cheddar cheese,

Direction:
Preheat the oven to broil. Place a 13-inch oven-proof pan over moderate flame. Spray the skillet with cooking spray. Fry the sliced bell pepper with mushrooms for 3 minutes. Include sausage, salt, and black pepper; reduce the heat to moderate and bake for 60 seconds; combine egg substitute with half-and-half; gently pour on sausage mixture. Bake for 6 minutes, covered. Garnish with cheddar cheese. Broil for 1–2 minutes or until the cheese melts. Cut the pizza into eight wedges. Serve and enjoy!

Nutrition: Fat: 6g, Net Carbs: 10g, Protein: 21g, Sodium: 588mg

SPINACH ALFREDO LASAGNA

Preparation time: 20 minutes **Cooking time:** 90 minutes **Serving:** 4

Ingredients:

- Cooking spray
- Egg, finely beaten,
- 1 Ricotta cheese,
- 15 ounces Frozen spinach, thawed,
- 10 ounces of Garlic cloves,
- 4 Pepper,
- 1/4 teaspoon Alfredo sauce,
- 15 ounces of Skimmed milk,
- 1/2 cup Lasagna noodles,
- 6 Shredded carrots,
- 2 cups Diced mushrooms,
- 2 cups Mozzarella cheese,
- 1/2 cup Parmesan cheese,

Direction:
Preheat the oven to 350°Fahrenheit. Cover a 2-quarter rectangular baking sheet lightly coated with cooking spray. Combine the following 5 ingredients inside a medium mixing bowl. Inside another bowl, mix Alfredo sauce with milk. Lay about 8 tablespoons of the milk mixture into the lower end of the baking sheet. Organize three portions of uncooked noodles within a coating over the sauce. Lay half of the prepared spinach mixture on the noodles, and garnish half of the shredded carrots and half of the diced mushrooms. Organize the rest of the uncooked noodles on the vegetables. Garnish with the leftover spinach mixture on top of the noodles.

Finish with the rest of the shredded carrots and mushrooms. Coat with the remaining milk mixture. Now sprinkle with mozzarella, then Parmesan cheese. Cover a sheet of aluminum foil evenly with cooking spray. Wrap the baking sheet in foil and spray side down. Cook for 60-70 minutes inside the oven. Uncover, and cook for another 16 to 22 minutes, or until the top is browned. Allow cooling for 22-minutes before serving. Enjoy!

Nutrition: Fat: 12g, Net Carbs: 24g, Protein: 16g, Sodium: 527mg

VEGETABLE MINESTRONE SOUP

Preparation time: 30 minutes **Cooking time:** 360 minutes **Serving:** 8

Ingredients:

- 1/2 cup Diced carrots,
- 4 Celery stalks, diced,
- 3 Diced red onion,
- 1 Chopped garlic clove,
- 3 Green beans flaked,
- 2-1/2 cups Red kidney beans,
- 15 ounces Tomatoes, undrained,
- 15 ounces of Vegetable broth,
- 6-1/2 cups Italian seasoning,
- 2 tablespoons Red pepper,
- 1 teaspoon Salt,
- 3/4 teaspoon Pepper,
- 1/2 teaspoon Diced zucchini,
- 1 Elbow pasta,
- 4 ounces Parmesan cheese,

Direction:
Combine the first 12 ingredients inside a 6- to 8-quart slow cooker. Cook on low flame for 7 to 8 hours, covered. Whisk in the zucchini, followed by pasta, and season with salt. Cover, and Cook, on low flame for 16 to 22 minutes more, otherwise until the pasta becomes soft. Serve cheese on top. Have fun!

Nutrition: Fat: 2g, Net Carbs: 41g, Protein: 11g, Sodium: 525mg

VEGAN CHILI WITH WHITE BEAN

Preparation time: 10 minutes **Cooking time:** 45 minutes **Serving:** 4

Ingredients:

- 2.5 tablespoons Canola oil,
- 1/4 cup Diced Anaheim pepper,
- 2 cups Diced onion,
- 1 Chopped garlic clove,
- 4 Quinoa, soaked,
- 1/2 cup Dried oregano,
- 4 teaspoons Ground cumin,
- 4 teaspoons Salt,
- 1 teaspoon Ground coriander,
- 1 teaspoon Ground pepper,
- 1 teaspoon Vegetable broth,
- 4 cups White beans,
- 15 ounces Chopped zucchini,
- 1 Diced cilantro,
- 1/4 cup Lime juice,

Direction:
Heat oil inside a big pot on a medium flame. Include the 1st three ingredients. Cook, while constantly stirring, for 6 to 8 minutes, or until the veggies are tender. Add quinoa, and oregano, followed by cumin, salt, coriander, and pepper; cook them while stirring until fragrant, about 1 minute. Whisk in the broth with beans. Get the water to a boil. Now reduce the flame and bring it to simmer. Cook, moderately covered, for 20 minutes, while stirring occasionally.

Include zucchini; cover, then cook for 11 to 16 minutes. Otherwise, the zucchini becomes tender, and the chili has thickened. Whisk in the cilantro with lime juice. End up serving with lime wedges.
Nutrition: Fat: 11g, Net Carbs: 36g, Protein: 9g, Sodium: 529mg

CAULIFLOWER FRIED RICE

Preparation time: 10 minutes **Cooking time:** 20 minutes **Serving:** 4

Ingredients:

- 1 head of cauliflower, tablespoons Sesame oil,
- , 1 cup Peas and carrots
- 1 tablespoon Soy sauce,
- 1/2 teaspoon Garlic powder,
- 1/4 teaspoon Black pepper,
- 2 Eggs, lightly beaten,
- 2 tablespoons Chopped scallions,

Direction:
In a food processor, pulse cauliflower till it is in small pieces, which resembles rice. Heat oil in a skillet over medium flame until hot; add the cauliflower, some peas, and the carrots now, and cook for 5 minutes. Mix with soy sauce, garlic powder, and chili. Coat a shallow skillet with the cooking spray, and then scramble eggs till smooth. Combine eggs and cauliflower in a mixing bowl. Cook for 5–7 minutes or until the cauliflower is soft. Serve with the scallions on top.
Nutrition: Fat: 6g, Net Carbs: 6g, Protein: 4g, Sodium: 162mg

ASPARAGUS PITA ROUNDS

Preparation time: 10 minutes **Cooking time:** 10 minutes **Serving:** 3
Ingredients:

- 2 cups Sliced asparagus,2 teaspoons Olive oil,
- 2 Garlic cloves, minced,
- 4 Pitas,
- 3 Plum tomatoes,
- 1 teaspoon Dried basil,1/4 teaspoonSalt,
- 6 tablespoons parmesan cheese,

Direction:
Preheat the oven to 450°F. Covered, steam asparagus for 2 minutes, or till crisp-tender. Drain after rinsing with cool water. Combine the oil and the garlic cloves. Brush pitas with olive oil. Place tomato slices and the asparagus on pita bread. Season with basil, some pepper, and salt to taste. Evenly sprinkle with the Parmesan cheese. Bake for about 7 to 8 minutes, until the edges are golden.
Nutrition: Fat: 5g, Net Carbs: 40g, Protein: 10g, Sodium: 601mg

SEAFOOD MARINARA PASTA

Preparation time: 25 minutes **Cooking time:** 30 minutes **Servings:** 4

Ingredients:

- 1 (16 Oz.) package linguine pasta
- 2 tbsp. olive oil, divided
- 4 cloves of garlic, minimum
- 1 small red onion, minimum
- 3 green onions, chopped
- 2 tomatoes, seeded and diced
- 1 (8 Oz.) can of crushed tomatoes
- 1 tbsp. tomato paste
- 1 tsp. dried oregano
- 1 tsp. ground thyme
- 2 lbs mussels, cleaned and debearded
- 1 lb uncooked medium shrimp, peeled and deveined
- 1 cup of dry white wine
- 2 tsp. lemon juice
- 1 lemon - cut into wedges for garnish

Directions:

A large saucepan of lightly salted water should be brought to a boil. It takes around 11 minutes to cook linguine at a boil until it is soft to the biting. In a colander in the sink, thoroughly drain. A skillet with one tbsp. Of olive oil in it should be heated to medium. Cook and stir the garlic and onion for about 5 minutes, or until the onion has softened and become translucent. One more tbsp. Olive oil is heated in a sizable skillet over low heat. Cook and stir the diced tomatoes and green onion until the tomatoes have softened. Add tomato paste, oregano, and thyme after stirring the onion and tomato mixture. 5 minutes of simmering. Mussels and shrimp are mixed, after which wine and lemon juice are added. Put a cover on it and turn the heat up. Cook the shrimp until they turn pink and the mussels open, then discard any that have not. Add lemon wedges as a garnish before serving over pasta.

Nutrition: 878 cals; protein 67.3g; carbs 104g; fat 16.8g; chole 236.1mg; sodium 938.6mg.

SEAFOOD LINGUINE

Preparation time: 25 minutes **Cooking time:** 30 minutes **Servings:** 4

Ingredients:

- 1 (16 Oz.) package linguine pasta
- ½ cup of thinly sliced red onion
- 3 tsp. garlic powder
- ¼ cup of olive oil
- 3 cups of milk
- 2 tsp. chopped fresh parsley
- ½ cup of chopped green bell pepper
- ½ cup of red bell pepper, chopped
- ½ cup of broccoli florets
- ½ cup of thinly sliced carrots
- 1 cup of sliced fresh mushrooms
- 1 cup of canned shrimp

- 1 cup of crab meat, drained
- 1 lb scallops
- 2 tbsp. all-purpose flour
- salt to taste
- ground black pepper to taste

Directions:
A large saucepan of lightly salted water should be brought to a boil. When the pasta is al dente, add the linguini and simmer for 6 to 8 minutes. Drain. Meanwhile, sauté the red onion and garlic in olive oil in a large skillet or electric frying pan. Add the milk once the onion is transparent. Cook until bubbles start to appear around the pan's edges. Stir in the parsley, green, and red bell pepper that has been diced, broccoli, carrots, mushrooms, shrimp, crab, and scallops. Remove 1/2 cup of milk from the mixture and add it to the flour in a small bowl. Until smooth, stir. Re-add to the skillet along with the seafood and veggies. Let the mixture thicken. To taste, add salt and pepper to the food. Overcooked and drained linguini noodles, drizzle seafood sauce. Serve hot.
Nutrition: 418 cals; protein 28.2g; carbs 52g; fat 11g; chole 68.7mg; sodium 242.5mg.

LEMON SEAFOOD RISOTTO

Preparation time: 30 minutes **Cooking time:** 25 minutes **Servings:** 6
Ingredients:

- 1 cup of Arborio rice
- 2 cups of low-sodium chicken broth, divided
- 2 tbsp. olive oil
- ½ lb bay scallops

- 1 large leek, cleaned and thinly sliced
- 2 cloves garlic, minimum
- 1 cup of dry white wine
- ½ lb medium shrimp, peeled and deveined
- 1 cup of fresh snow peas, trimmed and halved crosswise
- 1 medium red bell pepper, diced
- 3 tbsp. grated Parmesan cheese
- 2 tsp. dried basil
- 2 tbsp. lemon juice
- ground black pepper to taste

Directions:
Warm the olive oil over low heat in a sizable, heavy-bottomed saucepan. Cook and stir the leek and garlic for about five minutes, or until tender. Cook the rice for an additional five minutes while stirring constantly. 1 1/2 cups of chicken broth should be added. Stirring occasionally, and bring to a boil over high heat. Simmer, uncovered, for 5 minutes on medium-low heat, stirring regularly. Stirring continuously, simmer for about 5 more minutes with the remaining chicken broth and wine at medium heat. Add the red pepper, peas, shrimp, and scallops. Cook with constant stirring for about 5 minutes, or until seafood is cooked and the liquid is almost completely absorbed. Add Parmesan cheese, basil, lemon juice, and pepper after the rice is just soft and creamy.
Nutrition: 330 cals; protein 19.7g; carbs 39.6g; fat 6.5g; chole 73.5mg; sodium 201.5mg.

MEDITERRANEAN SEAFOOD SALAD

Preparation time: 15 minutes **Cooking time: 10** minutes **Servings:** 10
Ingredients:

- 1 ½ cups of dried small pasta shells
- 3 cups of imitation crab or lobster meat
- 2 stalks of celery, finely chopped
- ¾ cups of black olives
- 1 ½ cups of mayonnaise
- ⅓ cups of Catalina salad dressing
- 2 tsp. Worcestershire sauce
- 1 tbsp. hot sauce
- ¼ tsp. Dijon mustard
- 1 cups of cubed Cheddar cheese

Directions:
A large saucepan of lightly salted water should be brought to a boil. Add the pasta and cook for 8 to 10 minutes until al dente. Pasta should be drained and put in a big bowl. Crabmeat, celery, and olives are stirred in. Add the Worcestershire sauce, spicy sauce, Dijon, and Catalina dressing. Add Cheddar cheese, stir, then chill for at least one hour.
Nutrition: 448 cals; protein 9.9g; carbs 24.4g; fat 35.3g; chole 36.6mg; sodium 935.2mg.

BROWN RICE WITH TUNA, PEPPERS, AND ROCKET

Preparation time: 10 minutes **Cooking time:** 25 minutes **Serving:** 4

Ingredients:

- 7 once of brown rice
- 7 once of tuna in water
- 1 red pepper
- 1 yellow pepper
- 1 shallot
- 1 cup of rocket
- 2 tablespoons of olive oil
- 1 pinch of salt
- 1 pinch of black pepper

Directions:
Clean the peppers, remove the stalk, cut it in half and remove the seeds. Cut them into strips. Chop the shallot in a non-stick pan, heat the oil, and brown the chopped shallot for 3 minutes. Add the peppers and cook, add salt and pepper and cook until they become soft. In a pot of lightly salted boiling water, cook the rice for about 15 minutes, drain it flat and mix it with the peppers, the tuna drained from the water, and the chopped rocket.

Nutrition: calories: 226 / fat: 8 / protein: 17 / carbs: 25 /

Coo ANo PUMPKIN FISHBALLS

Preparation time: 10 minutes **Cooking time:** 25 minutes **Serving:** 4

Ingredients:

- 7 once of cod
- 1 cup boiled pumpkin cubes
- 1 cup unsweetened soy yogurt
- 1 tablespoon of mustard
- 5 tablespoons of grated wholemeal bread
- 3 tablespoons of corn flour
- 5 tablespoons of olive oil
- 1 tablespoon of chopped parsley
- 1 pinch of salt
- 1 pinch of pepper

Directions:

Put the yogurt, mustard, and parsley in the mixer and chop. Set the sauce aside. In a non-stick pan with a tablespoon of oil, cook the cod for 5 minutes and then chop it coarsely. Mash the pumpkin with a fork, add the cod and a tablespoon of oil, a pinch of salt and pepper, and a tablespoon of breadcrumbs. Mix the ingredients well and shape them into balls with your hands. Dip the balls in the cornmeal mixed with the breadcrumbs and place them on a baking sheet lined with parchment paper. Heat the oven to 400° F and bake for 10 minutes. Serve with the sauce.

Nutrition: calories: 233 / fat: 13 / protein: 16 / carbs: 3 /

MACKEREL WITH SESAME AND SOY SPROUTS

Preparation time: 15 minutes **Cooking time:** 10 minutes **Serving:** 5

Ingredients:

- 1 lb of mackerel fillets in oil
- 2 yellow peppers
- 2 cloves of garlic
- 7 once of red beans
- 1 tablespoon of capers
- 1 cup of bean sprouts
- 1 organic lemon
- 1 tablespoon of sesame seeds
- 2 tablespoons of olive oil
- 1 pinch of salt
- 1 pinch of black pepper

Directions:
Chop the garlic. In a non-stick pan, heat a tablespoon of olive oil. Clean the peppers by removing the stalk, cutting them in two, and removing the seeds inside. Cut the peppers into strips. Sauté the garlic in the oil for a minute, then add the peppers, capers, and pepper and cook until soft. Crumble the mackerel fillets with your hands after draining them from the excess oil and mix with the sesame seeds. In a bowl, combine the mackerel, peppers, and bean sprouts and mix well.

Nutrition: calories: 346 / fat: 22 / protein: 20 / carbs: 17 /

QUINOA WITH TUNA PESTO

Preparation time: 10 minutes **Cooking time:** 20 minutes **Serving:** 4

Ingredients:

- 1 lb of quinoa
- 7 once of tuna in water
- 3 once of feta
- 1 tomato
- 1 cucumber
- 1 tablespoon of hazelnuts
- 1 tablespoon of chopped basil
- 1 pinch of salt
- 1 pinch of cayenne pepper
- 1 tablespoon of olive oil

Directions:
Cook the quinoa in plenty of lightly salted boiling water for 15-20 minutes and drain well. Put the tuna in the blender with the feta, hazelnuts, basil, and olive oil and blend until smooth. Wash and dice the tomato. Remove the peel from the cucumber and cut it into thin slices. Combine the quinoa with the vegetables and the sauce and mix well.

Nutrition: calories: 262 / fat: 9 / protein: 22 / carbs: 25 /

OYSTER AND MUSHROOM SOUP

Preparation time: 10 minutes **Cooking time:** 50 minutes **Serving:** 6

Ingredients:

- 15 oysters
- 1 teaspoon of oregano
- 1 teaspoon of thyme
- 1 cup of white mushrooms
- 2 cups low sodium vegetable broth
- 1 onion
- 1 leek
- 1 yellow potato
- 1 tablespoon of coconut butter

Directions:

In a non-stick pan, melt the coconut butter, brown the chopped onion and leek. Add the sliced mushrooms, mix and after a minute, add the vegetable broth and cook for 20 minutes over moderate heat. Add the thyme and oregano. Cut the potato into cubes, add it and cook for another 20 minutes. Wash the oysters well, and put them in a saucepan with the lid on low heat to make them open. Once opened, extract the mollusks and filter the liquid they have released with a strainer. Add the juice to the mushrooms and potatoes. Cook for another 3 minutes, add the oysters, mix and serve.

Nutrition: calories: 101 / fat: 8 / protein: 7 / carbs: 9 /

SALMON WITH ROCKET PESTO

Preparation time: 10 minutes **Cooking time:** 10 minutes **Servings:** 4

Ingredients:

- 4 wild salmon fillets
- 2 tablespoons of parsley
- 1 cup of rocket
- 2 cloves of garlic
- 1 organic lemon
- 3 tablespoons of olive oil
- 5 tablespoons of cashews
- 1 pinch of salt
- 1 pinch of cayenne pepper

Directions:

Wash and put the rocket, garlic, cashews, a pinch of salt and a tablespoon of oil in a mixer and blend well. Put the pesto obtained in the refrigerator. Wash, the salmon, brush it with oil and place it on a baking sheet covered with parchment paper at 400° F for about 10 minutes. Remove the salmon from the oven and cover it with the pesto.

Nutrition: Calories: 346kcal; Fat: 27g; Protein: 18g; Carbs: 7g

CABBAGE WITH ANCHOVIES

Preparation time: 10 minutes **Cooking time:** 0 minutes **Servings:** 2

Ingredients:

- 2 cups of boiled cabbage
- 2 tablespoons of capers
- 5 anchovies in oil
- 2 tomatoes
- 1 chili
- 2 tablespoons of olive oil
- 1 pinch of salt
- 1 pinch of cayenne pepper
- 1 tablespoon of chopped fresh parsley

Directions:

Mix the anchovies cut into small pieces in a bowl, the chopped chili pepper, the parsley, the whole capers, the diced tomatoes, the oil, the salt, and the pepper. Add the cabbage and mix again.

Nutrition: Calories: 257kcal; Fat: 19g; Protein: 12g; Carbs: 11g

WHOLEMEAL PASTA WITH SARDE

Preparation time: 5 minutes **Cooking time:** 15 minutes **Servings:** 3
Ingredients:

- 7 once of wholemeal pasta
- 2 leeks
- 1 basket of radicchio
- 8 clean sardines
- 2 tablespoons of olive oil
- 1 pinch of salt
- 1 pinch of pepper

Directions:
Clean and cut the leeks into thin slices. In a non-stick pan, sauté the leeks with the oil, the chopped radicchio, and the sardines cut into small pieces, add the salt and pepper and cook, stirring, for 10 minutes. In a pot with plenty of lightly salted boiling water, cook the pasta for the cooking time indicated on the package, drain well and season with the prepared sardine sauce.
Nutrition: Calories: 237kcal; Fat: 11g; Protein: 13g; Carbs: 22g

SALMON SALAD

Preparation time: 5 minutes **Cooking time:** 10 minutes **Servings:** 2

Ingredients:

- 7 once of smoked wild salmon
- 3 once cremini mushrooms
- 1 cup of boiled broccoli
- 2 tablespoons of chopped parsley
- 2 tablespoons of olive oil
- 1 pinch of salt
- 1 pinch of cayenne pepper
- 1 organic lemon

Directions:

Cut the salmon into strips and marinate in the lemon juice. Wash, the mushrooms, cut them into skinny slices and add them to the salmon. In a non-stick pan, heat the oil and pour the broccoli. Add the salt, pepper, and brown for 5 minutes. Drain the lemon juice from the salmon and mushrooms and put them in a bowl. Add the broccoli and parsley, and serve.

Nutrition: Calories: 298kcal; Fat: 19g; Protein: 26g; Carbs: 4g

FLAVORS LIME SHRIMP

Preparation Time: 10 minutes **Cooking Time:** 4 minutes **Serve: 4**
Ingredients:

- 1 lb shrimp, peeled & deveined
- ¼ cup fresh cilantro, chopped
- 1 tbsp lime juice
- 2 garlic cloves, minced
- 1 tbsp canola oil
- ¼ tsp paprika
- 1 tsp chili powder
- Pepper
- Salt

Directions:
Heat oil in a pan over medium-high heat. Add shrimp and season with chili powder, paprika, pepper, and salt, and cook for 2 minutes or until the shrimp turns pink in color. Add garlic and cook for a minute. Stir in cilantro and lime juice. Serve and enjoy.
Nutrition: Calories 171 Fat 5.6 g Carbohydrates 3.3 g Sugar 0.3 g Protein 26 g Cholesterol 239 mg

ASIAN SALMON

Preparation Time: 10 minutes **Cooking Time:** 15 minutes **Serve:** 4

Ingredients:

- 4 salmon fillets
- 2 tbsp soy sauce
- 2 tbsp honey
- 1 tsp ginger, minced
- 2 tbsp coriander
- 1 tbsp olive oil
- 1 lime zest
- ¼ tsp pepper

Directions:
Preheat the oven to 225° F. Mix oil, ginger, coriander, and zest in a small bowl. Place salmon fillets into a baking dish and brush with oil mixture. Bake in preheated oven for 15 minutes. Mix honey and pepper and drizzle over-baked salmon with soy sauce. Serve and enjoy.
Nutrition: Calories 304 Fat 14.5 g Carbohydrates 9.8 g Sugar 8.8 g Protein 35.1 g Cholesterol 78 mg

BROILED TURMERIC FISH

Preparation Time: 10 minutes **Cooking Time:** 10 minutes **Serve:** 4
Ingredients:

- 4 red snapper fish fillets
- 1/8 tsp cayenne
- ½ tsp ground turmeric
- 1 tsp ground coriander
- 2 tbsp olive oil
- 1 tbsp ginger, grated
- 2 tbsp fresh lime juice
- Pepper
- Salt

Directions:
Preheat the broiler. Mix oil, lime juice, ginger, coriander, turmeric, cayenne, pepper, and salt in a small bowl. Brush fish fillets with oil mixture and place onto the greased broiler pan and broil for 8-10 minutes. Serve and enjoy.
Nutrition: Calories 362 Fat 21.2 g Carbohydrates 28 g Sugar 1.4 g Protein 16.2 g Cholesterol 49 mg

SPICED MAHI MAHI

Preparation Time: 10 minutes **Cooking Time:** 8 minutes **Serve:** 2
Ingredients:

- 2 mahi-mahi fillets
- 2 tbsp olive oil
- 1 tsp rosemary
- 2 tsp thyme
- 2 tsp coriander
- 1 tsp turmeric
- Salt

Directions:
In a baking dish, place fish fillets and coat them with turmeric, coriander, thyme, rosemary, and salt. Cover the container and place in the fridge for 1 hour. Heat oil in a pan over medium heat. Place marinated fish fillets in a hot pan and cook for 4 minutes on each side. Serve and enjoy.
Nutrition: Calories 218 Fat 15.2 g Carbohydrates 1.7 g Sugar 0.1 g Protein 19.1 g Cholesterol 86 mg

HEALTHY TUNA SALAD

Preparation Time: 10 minutes **Cooking Time:** 5 minutes **Serve:** 2
Ingredients:

- 6 oz can tuna, drained & flaked
- 1 fresh lime juice
- 2 tbsp unsweetened dried cranberries
- 1 tbsp Dijon mustard
- 2 tbsp onion, minced
- 3 tbsp mayonnaise
- Pepper
- Salt

Directions:
Add tuna and remaining ingredients into the bowl and mix until well combined. Cover and place in the fridge for 1 hour. Serve and enjoy.
Nutrition: Calories 117 Fat 5.5 g Carbohydrates 5.2 g Sugar 1.8 g Protein 11.3 g Cholesterol 17 mg

CHILI LIME SALMON

Preparation Time: 10 minutes **Cooking Time:** 10 minutes **Serve:** 4
Ingredients:

- 4 salmon fillets
- ¼ cup fresh lime juice
- 1 tbsp canola oil
- 1 tbsp honey
- 1 tsp ground cumin
- ½ tsp chili powder
- ¼ tsp smoked paprika
- 2 tbsp olive oil
- 1 tbsp garlic, crushed
- Salt

Directions:
Mix lime juice, honey, cumin, chili powder, paprika, olive oil, garlic, and salt in a mixing bowl. Add fish fillets and coat well with lime mixture. Cover bowl and set aside for 15 minutes. Heat canola oil in a pan over medium heat. Place marinated fish fillets in a pan and cook for 5 minutes on each side. Serve and enjoy.
Nutrition: Calories 348 Fat 21.6 g Carbohydrates 5.7 g Sugar 4.4 g Protein 34.8 g Cholesterol 78 mg

BAKED FISH FILLETS

Preparation Time: 10 minutes **Cooking Time:** 20 minutes **Serve:** 2
Ingredients:

- 2 salmon fillets
- ¼ tsp garlic powder
- 1 tsp turmeric
- 3 tbsp olive oil
- ½ lemon juice
- Pepper
- Salt

Directions:
Preheat the oven to 425° F. Place fish fillets into the baking dish. Mix the remaining ingredients, pour over fish fillets, and marinate for 20 minutes. Place in oven and bake for 15-20 minutes. Serve and enjoy.
Nutrition: Calories 423 Fat 32.2 g Carbohydrates 1.2 g Sugar 0.4 g Protein 34.8 g Cholesterol 78 mg

BROCCOLI & CHICKEN STIR-FRY

Preparation time: 5 minutes **Cooking time:** 20 minutes **Serves** 4
Ingredients:

- 2 cups broccoli florets
- 1 ½ lb chicken breasts, cubed
- ½ onion, chopped
- Sea salt and pepper to taste
- 3 tbsp extra-virgin olive oil
- 3 garlic cloves, minced

Direction:
Warm the olive oil in a skillet over medium heat. Add the broccoli, chicken, garlic, onion, and stir-fry for about 8 minutes, or until the chicken is golden browned and cooked through. Season with salt and pepper. Serve.
Nutrition: Cal: 345; Fat 13g; Carbs 4g; Protein 13g

CHICKEN A LA TUSCANA

Preparation time: 5 minutes **Cooking time:** 25 minutes **Serves** 4
Ingredients:

- 2 cups cherry tomatoes
- 4 chicken breast halves
- 1 tsp garlic powder
- Sea salt and pepper to taste
- 2 tbsp extra-virgin olive oil
- ½ cup sliced green olives
- 1 eggplant, chopped
- ¼ cup dry white wine

Direction:
Pound the chicken breasts with a meat tenderizer until half an inch thick. Rub them with garlic powder, salt, and ground black pepper. Warm the olive oil in a skillet over medium heat. Add the chicken and cook for 14-16 minutes, flipping halfway through the cooking time. Transfer to a plate and cover with aluminum foil. Add the tomatoes, olives, and eggplant to the skillet and sauté for 4 minutes or until the vegetables are soft. Add the white wine to the skillet and simmer for 1 minute. Remove the aluminum foil, top the chicken with the vegetables and their juices, and then serve warm.
Nutrition: Cal: 170; Fat 10g; Carbs 8g; Protein 7g

BAKED BASIL CHICKEN

Preparation time: 5 minutes **Cooking time:** 45 minutes **Serves** 4
Ingredients:

- 2 garlic cloves, sliced
- 1 white onion, chopped
- 14 oz tomatoes, chopped
- 2 tbsp chopped rosemary
- Sea salt and pepper to taste
- 4 skinless chicken thighs
- 1 lb peeled pumpkin, cubed
- 1 tbsp extra virgin olive oil
- 2 tbsp basil leaves

Direction:
Preheat your oven to 375°F. Warm the olive oil in a skillet over medium heat. Add the garlic and onion and sauté for 5 minutes or until fragrant. Add the tomatoes, rosemary, salt, and pepper and cook for 15 minutes or until slightly thickened. Arrange the chicken thighs and pumpkin cubes on a baking sheet, then pour the mixture in the skillet over the chicken and sweet potatoes. Stir to coat well. Pour in enough water to cover the chicken and sweet potatoes. Bake for 20 minutes. Top with basil.
Nutrition: Cal: 295; Fat 9g; Carbs 32g; Protein 21g

GRILLED LEMON CHICKEN

Preparation time: 10 minutes **Cooking time:** 12 to 14 minutes
Serves: 2
Ingredients:

- 1 (4-ounce / 113-g) boneless, skinless chicken breasts

Marinade:

- 4 tablespoons freshly squeezed lemon juice
- 2 tablespoons olive oil, plus more for greasing the grill grates
- 1 teaspoon dried basil
- 1 teaspoon paprika
- ½ teaspoon dried thyme
- ¼ teaspoon salt
- ¼ teaspoon garlic powder

Directions:
Make the marinade:
Whisk together the lemon juice, olive oil, basil, paprika, thyme, salt, and garlic powder in a large bowl until well combined. Add the chicken breasts to the bowl and let marinate for at least 30 minutes. When ready to cook, preheat the grill to medium-high heat. Lightly grease the grill grates with olive oil. Discard the marinade and arrange the chicken breasts on the grill grates. Grill for 12 to 14 minutes, flipping the chicken halfway through, or until a meat thermometer inserted in the center of the chicken reaches 165°F (74°C). Let the chicken cool for 5 minutes and serve warm.
Nutrition: calories: 251 | fat: 15.5g | protein: 27.3g | carbs: 1.9g

SPICED ROAST CHICKEN

Preparation time: 10 minutes **Cooking time:** 35 minutes **Serves**: 6
Ingredients:

- 1 teaspoon garlic powder
- 1 teaspoon ground paprika
- ½ teaspoon ground cumin
- ½ teaspoon ground coriander
- ½ teaspoon salt
- ¼ teaspoon ground cayenne pepper
- 6 chicken legs
- 1 teaspoon extra-virgin olive oil

Directions:
Preheat the oven to 400°F. In a small bowl, combine the garlic powder, paprika, cumin, coriander, salt, and cayenne pepper. Rub the spices all over the chicken legs until wholly coated on a clean work surface. Heat the olive oil in an ovenproof skillet over medium heat. Add the chicken thighs and sear each side for 8 to 10 minutes, until the skin is crispy and browned. Transfer the skillet to the preheated oven and continue cooking for 10 to 15 minutes, or until the juices run clear and it registers an internal temperature of 165°F (74°C). Remove from the heat and serve on plates.
Nutrition: calories: 275 | fat: 15.6g | protein: 30.3g | carbs: 0.9g

CHICKEN BRUSCHETTA BURGERS

Preparation time: 10 minutes **Cooking time:** 16 minutes **Serves:** 2
Ingredients:

- 1 tablespoon olive oil
- 2 garlic cloves, minced
- 3 tablespoons finely minced onion
- 1 teaspoon dried basil
- 3 tablespoons minced sun-dried tomatoes packed in olive oil
- 8 ounces (227 g) of ground chicken breast
- ¼ teaspoon salt
- 3 pieces of small Mozzarella balls, minced

Directions:
Heat the olive oil in a nonstick skillet over medium-high heat. Add the garlic and onion and sauté for 5 minutes until tender. Stir in the basil. Remove from the skillet to a medium bowl. Add the tomatoes, ground chicken, and salt and stir until incorporated. Mix in the Mozzarella balls. Divide the chicken mixture in half and form into two burgers, each about ¾-inch thick. Heat the same skillet over medium-high heat and add the burgers. Cook each side for 5 to 6 minutes, or until they reach an internal temperature of 165°F (74°C). Serve warm.
Nutrition: calories: 300 | fat: 17.0g | protein: 32.2g | carbs: 6.0g

QUICK CHICKEN SALAD WRAPS

Preparation time: 15 minutes **Cooking time:** 0 minutes **Serves:** 2
Ingredients:
Tzatziki Sauce:

- ½ cup plain Greek yogurt
- 1 tablespoon freshly squeezed lemon juice
- Pinch garlic powder
- 1 teaspoon dried dill
- Salt and freshly ground black pepper to taste
- 1 scallion, chopped
- ¼ cup pitted black olives

Salad Wraps:

- 2 (8-inch) whole-grain pita bread
- 1 cup shredded chicken meat
- 2 cups mixed greens
- 2 roasted red bell peppers, thinly sliced
- ½ English cucumber, peeled and thinly sliced

Directions:
Make the tzatziki sauce:
Whisk together the yogurt, lemon juice, garlic powder, dill, salt, and pepper until creamy and smooth. Make the salad wraps: Place the pita bread on a clean work surface and spoon ¼ cup of the tzatziki sauce onto each piece of pita bread, spreading it all over. Top with the shredded chicken, mixed greens, red pepper slices, cucumber slices, and black olives, finished with chopped scallion. Roll the salad wraps and enjoy.

Nutrition: calories: 428 | fat: 10.6g | protein: 31.1g | carbs: 50.9g

CHICKEN WITH ASIAN VEGETABLES

Preparation time: 10 minutes **Cooking time**: 20 minutes **Servings:** 8

Ingredients:

- 2 Tablespoons canola oil
- 6 boneless chicken breasts
- 1 cup low-sodium chicken broth
- 3 Tablespoons reduced-sodium soy sauce
- ¼ tsp. crushed red pepper flakes
- 1 garlic clove, crushed
- 1 can (8ounces) water chestnuts, sliced and rinsed (optional)
- ½ cup sliced green onions
- 1 cup chopped red or green bell pepper
- 1 cup chopped celery
- ¼ cup cornstarch
- 1/3 cup water
- 3 cups cooked white rice
- ½ large chicken breast for one chicken thigh

Directions:

Warm oil in a skillet and dark-colored chicken on all sides. Add chicken to a slow cooker with the remainder of the fixings aside from cornstarch and water. Spread and cook on LOW for 6 to 8 hours. Following 6-8 hours, independently blend cornstarch and cold water until smooth. Gradually include into the slow cooker. At that point,

turn on high for about 15mins until thickened. Don't close the top on the slow cooker to enable steam to leave. Serve.
Nutrition: Calories: 415Kcal; Protein: 20g; Carbohydrates: 36g; Fat: 20g

CHICKEN AND VEGGIE SOUP

Preparation time: 15 minutes **Cooking time:** 25 minutes **Servings:** 8

Ingredients:

- 4 cups cooked and chopped chicken
- 7 cups reduced-sodium chicken broth
- 1-pound froze white corn
- 1 medium onion diced
- 4 cloves garlic minced
- 2 carrots peeled and diced
- 2 celery stalks chopped
- 2 tsp. oregano
- 2 tsp. curry powder
- ½ tsp. black pepper

Directions:
Include all fixings into the slow cooker. Cook on LOW for 8 hours
Serve over cooked white rice.
Nutrition: Calories: 220Kcal; Protein: 24g; Carbohydrates: 19g; Fat: 7g

TURKEY SAUSAGES

Preparation time: 10 minutes **Cooking time:** 10 minutes **Servings:** 2

Ingredients:

- 1/4 tsp. salt
- 1/8 tsp. garlic powder
- 1/8 tsp. onion powder
- One tsp. fennel seed
- 1 pound 7% Fat: ground turkey

Directions:

Press the fennel seed and put together turkey with fennel seed, garlic, onion powder, and salt in a small cup. Cover the bowl and refrigerate overnight. Prepare the turkey with seasoning into different portions with a circle form and press them into patties ready to be cooked. Cook at medium heat until browned. Cook it for 1 to 2 minutes per side and serve them hot. Enjoy!

Nutrition: Calories: 55Kcal; Protein: 3g; Carbohydrates: 5g; Fat: 7g

ROSEMARY CHICKEN

Preparation time: 10 minutes **Cooking time:** 10 minutes **Servings:** 2

Ingredients:

- 2 zucchinis
- 1 carrot
- 1 tsp. dried rosemary
- 4 chicken breasts
- 1/2 bell pepper
- 1/2 red onion
- 8 garlic cloves
- Olive oil
- 1/4 tbs. ground pepper

Directions:

Prepare the oven and preheat it at 375 °F (or 200°C). Slice both zucchini and carrots and add bell pepper, onion, garlic, and put everything adding oil in a 13" x 9" pan. Spread the pepper over everything and roast for about 10 minutes. Meanwhile, lift the chicken skin and spread black pepper and rosemary on the flesh. Take away the vegetable pan from the oven and add the chicken, returning it to the oven for about 30 more minutes. Serve and enjoy!

Nutrition: Calories: 215 Protein: 2g; Carbohydrates: 4g; Fat: 6.3g

SMOKEY TURKEY CHILI

Preparation time: 5 minutes **Cooking time:** 45 minutes **Servings:** 8

Ingredients:

- 12ounce lean ground turkey
- 1/2 red onion, chopped
- 2 cloves garlic, crushed and chopped
- ½ tsp. of smoked paprika
- ½ tsp. of chili powder
- ½ tsp. of dried thyme
- ¼ cup reduced-sodium beef stock
- ½ cup of water
- 1 ½ cups baby spinach leaves, washed
- 3 wheat tortillas

Directions:
Brown the ground beef in a dry skillet over medium-high heat. Add in the red onion and garlic. Sauté the onion until it goes clear. Transfer the contents of the skillet to the slow cooker. Add the remaining ingredients and simmer on low for 30–45 minutes. Stir through the spinach for the last few minutes to wilt. Slice tortillas and gently toast under the broiler until slightly crispy. Serve on top of the turkey chili.

Nutrition: Calories: 93.5Kcal; Protein: 8g; Carbohydrates: 3g; Fat: 5.5g

PINEAPPLE CRANBERRY CHICKEN

Preparation time: 5 minutes **Cooking time:** 40 minutes **Servings:** 8

Ingredients:

- 4 lbs skinless, boneless chicken breast halves
- 1 (16 Oz.) can of whole cranberry sauce
- 1 (20 Oz.) can of crushed pineapple, drained
- ½ tsp. ground cinnamon

Directions:
Set oven to 375° F. Put the chicken in a 9x13-inch baking dish that has been lightly greased, and poke with a fork. Chicken is covered with cranberry sauce, pineapple, and cinnamon. Cover the dish and bake it for 25 minutes in a preheated oven. Bake for 15 minutes, or until chicken is thoroughly done, without the cover (juices run clear).

Nutrition: 374 cals; protein 47.5g; carbs 31.9g; fat 5.5g; chole 129.4mg; sodium 125.4mg.

CHICKEN BREASTS AND MUSHROOMS

Preparation time: 5 minutes **Cooking time:** 30 minutes **Servings:** 6
Ingredients:

- 3 lbs. chicken breasts, skinless
- 1 yellow onion, chopped boneless
- 1 garlic clove, minced
- A pinch of salt and black pepper
- 10 mushrooms, chopped
- 1 tbsp. olive oil
- 2 red bell peppers, chopped

Directions:
Put the chicken in a baking dish, add onion, garlic, salt, pepper, mushrooms, oil, and bell peppers. Mix briefly and bake in the oven at 425°F for 25minutes. Enjoy!
Nutrition: Calories 285 Total Fat 11g Carbs 13g Protein 16g Fiber 1g

CHICKEN AND BRUSSELS SPROUTS

Preparation Time: 10 minutes **Cooking Time:** 10 minutes
Servings: 4
Ingredients:

- 1 cored, peeled, and chopped apple
- 1 chopped yellow onion
- 1 tbsp. organic olive oil
- 3 c. shredded Brussels sprouts
- 1 lb. ground chicken meat
- Black pepper

Directions:
Heat a pan while using oil over medium-high heat, add chicken, stir and brown for 5 minutes. Add Brussels sprouts, onion, black pepper, and apple, stir, cook for 10 minutes, divide into bowls and serve. Enjoy!
Nutrition: Calories: 200Fat: 8 g Carbs: 13 g Protein: 9 g Sugars: 3 g Sodium: 194 mg

CHERRY BALSAMIC CHICKEN BREASTS

Preparation time: 10 minutes **Cooking Time:** 40 Minutes **Servings: 4**
Ingredients:

- 2 tbsp parsley, chopped
- 4 chicken breasts
- 2 scallions, sliced
- 2 tbsp coconut oil
- ¾ cup chicken broth
- 1 tbsp balsamic vinegar
- ½ cup dried cherries
- Sea salt and pepper to taste

Directions:
Preheat your oven to 375ºF. Melt the coconut oil in a large skillet over medium heat. Season the chicken with salt and pepper. Place the chicken in the pan and brown it on both sides for 3 minutes per side. Add the scallions, chicken broth, balsamic vinegar, and dried cherries. Cover with an ovenproof lid or aluminum foil and place the pan in the oven. Bake for 20 minutes or until the chicken is cooked through. Top with parsley.
Nutrition: Per Serving: Calories: 380;Fat: 15g;Protein: 42g;Carbs: 17g.

COCONUT-CURRY-CASHEW CHICKEN

Preparation time: 15 minutes **Cooking time:** 7 to 8 hours on low
Serves 4
Ingredients:

- 1½ cups chicken bone broth
- 1 (14-ounce) can of full-fat coconut milk
- 1 teaspoon garlic powder
- 1 tablespoon red curry paste
- 1 teaspoon sea salt
- ½ teaspoon freshly ground black pepper
- ½ teaspoon coconut sugar
- 2 pounds boneless, skinless chicken breasts
- 1½ cup unsalted cashews
- ½ cup diced white onion

Direction:
In a medium bowl, combine the broth, coconut milk, garlic powder, red curry paste, salt, pepper, and coconut sugar. Stir well. Put the chicken, cashews, and onion in the slow cooker. Pour the coconut milk mixture on top. Cover the oven and set it to low. Cook for 7 to 8 hours, or until the internal temperature of the chicken reaches 165°F on a meat thermometer and the juices run clear. Shred the chicken with a fork, and mix it into the cooking liquid. You can also remove the chicken from the broth and chop it with a knife into bite-size pieces before returning it to the slow cooker. Serve.
Nutrition: Calories: 714; Total Fat: 43g; Total Carbs: 21g; Sugar: 5g; Fiber: 3g; Protein: 57g; Sodium: 1,606mg

SESAME MISO CHICKEN

Preparation Time: 10 minutes **Cooking time:** 4 Hours **Serves** 4
Ingredients:

- ¼ cup white miso
- 2 tablespoons coconut oil, melted
- 2 tablespoons honey
- 1 tablespoon unseasoned rice wine vinegar
- 2 garlic cloves, thinly sliced
- 1 teaspoon minced fresh ginger root
- 1 cup chicken broth
- 8 boneless, skinless chicken thighs
- 2 scallions, sliced
- 1 tablespoon sesame seeds

Direction:
In a slow cooker, combine the miso, coconut oil, honey, rice wine vinegar, garlic, and ginger root, mixing well. Add the chicken and toss to combine. Cover and cook on high for 4 hours. Transfer the chicken and sauce to a serving dish. Garnish with the scallions and sesame seeds, and serve.

Nutrition: Calories: 320; Total Fat: 15g; Total Carbohydrates: 17g; Sugar: 11g; Fiber: 1g; Protein: 32g; Sodium: 1,020mg

GINGER TURKEY BURGERS

Preparation Time: 10 minutes **Cooking time:** 10 minutes **Serves** 4
Ingredients:

- 1½ pounds of ground turkey
- 1 large egg, lightly beaten
- 2 tablespoons coconut flour (or almond flour)
- ½ cup finely chopped onion
- 1 garlic clove, minced
- 2 teaspoons minced fresh ginger root
- 1 tablespoon fresh cilantro
- 1 teaspoon salt
- ¼ teaspoon freshly ground black pepper
- 1 tablespoon extra-virgin olive oil

Direction:
In a medium bowl, mix the ground turkey, egg, flour, onion, garlic, ginger root, cilantro, salt, and pepper. Form the turkey mixture into four patties. Heat the olive oil in a large skillet over medium-high heat. Cook the burgers, flipping once, until firm to the touch, 3 to 4 minutes on each side. Serve.
Nutrition: Calories: 320; Total Fat: 20g; Total Carbohydrates: 2g; Sugar: 1g; Fiber: <1g; Protein: 34g; Sodium: 720mg

MUSHROOM TURKEY THIGHS

Preparation Time: 15 minutes **Cooking time**: 4 Hours **Serves** 4
Ingredients:

- 1 tablespoon extra-virgin olive oil
- 2 turkey thighs
- 2 cups button or cremini mushrooms, sliced
- 1 large onion, sliced
- 1 garlic clove, sliced
- 1 rosemary sprig
- 1 teaspoon salt
- ¼ teaspoon freshly ground black pepper
- 2 cups chicken broth
- ½ cup dry red wine

Direction:
Drizzle the olive oil into a slow cooker. Add the turkey thighs, mushrooms, onion, garlic, rosemary sprig, salt, and pepper. Pour in the chicken broth and wine. Cover and cook on high for 4 hours. Remove and discard the rosemary sprig. Use a slotted spoon to transfer the thighs to a plate and allow them to cool for several minutes for easier handling. Cut the meat from the bones, stir the meat into the mushrooms, and serve.
Nutrition: Calories: 280; Total Fat: 9g; Total Carbohydrates: 3g; Sugar: 1g; Fiber: <1g; Protein: 43g; Sodium: 850mg

BEEF MEATLOAF WITH HORSERADISH

Preparation time: 5 minutes **Cooking time:** 70 minutes **Serves** 4
Ingredients:

- 1 ½ lb ground beef
- 1 egg
- ½ cup almond flour
- ½ cup chopped sweet onion
- 1 tbsp chopped fresh basil
- 1 tsp Dijon mustard
- 1 tsp grated horseradish
- ⅛ tsp sea salt

Direction:
Preheat your oven to 350°F. In a mixing bowl, combine the ground beef, almond flour, onion, egg, basil, mustard, horseradish, and sea salt until well mixed. Press the meatloaf mixture into a loaf pan. Bake for about 1 hour until cooked through. Remove the meatloaf from the oven and let it rest for 10 minutes before slicing.
Nutrition: Cal 405; Fat 17g; Carbs 4g; Protein 55g

HERBED LAMB ROAST WITH POTATOES

Preparation time: 5 minutes **Cooking time:** 70 minutes **Serves** 4
Ingredients:

- 1 (3-lb) lamb leg
- 2 cups chicken broth
- 1 tsp dried sage
- 1 tsp dried marjoram
- 1 tsp dried thyme
- 1 bay leaf, crushed
- 3 garlic cloves, minced
- 1 lb sweet potatoes, cubed
- 2 tbsp olive oil
- 3 tbsp arrowroot powder
- Sea salt and pepper to taste

Direction:
Heat the oil in your Instant Pot on "Sauté ."Combine the herbs with salt and pepper and rub the mixture into the meat. Brown the lamb on all sides. Pour the broth around the meat, close the lid, and cook for 60 minutes on "Manual." Release the pressure quickly and add the potatoes. Close the lid and cook for 10 more minutes. Transfer the meat and potatoes to a plate. Combine 1 cup of water and arrowroot and stir the mixture into the pot sauce. Pour the gravy over the meat and potatoes.
Nutrition: Cal 740; Fat 57g; Carbs 1g; Protein 57g

TOMATO BEEF MEATBALLS

Preparation time: 5 minutes **Cooking time:** 8 hours 15 minutes
Serves 6
Ingredients:

- 1 ½ lb ground beef
- 1 can crushed tomatoes
- 1 small onion, minced
- 1 large egg
- ¼ cup minced mushrooms
- 1 tsp garlic powder
- Sea salt and pepper to taste
- ½ tsp dried thyme
- ¼ tsp ground ginger
- ¼ tsp red pepper flakes

Direction:
In a large bowl, combine the ground beef, egg, onion, mushrooms, garlic powder, salt, pepper, thyme, ginger, and red pepper flakes. Mix well. Form the beef mixture into about 12 meatballs. Pour the tomatoes into your slow cooker. Gently arrange the meatballs on top. Cover the oven and set it to "Low ."Cook for 8 hours.
Nutrition: Cal 130; Fat 9g; Carbs 2g; Protein 10g

BEEF BOLOGNESE

Preparation time: 5 minutes **Cooking time:** 8 hours 15 minutes
Serves 4
Ingredients:

- 1 lb ground beef
- 1 can diced tomatoes
- 3 garlic cloves, minced
- 1 tbsp extra-virgin olive oil
- 1 chopped onion
- 1 chopped celery stalk
- 1 chopped carrot
- 1 tbsp white wine vinegar
- ⅛ tsp ground nutmeg
- ½ cup red wine
- ½ tsp red pepper flakes
- Sea salt and pepper to taste

Direction:
Grease your slow cooker with olive oil. Add onion, garlic, celery, carrot, ground beef, tomatoes, vinegar, nutmeg, wine, pepper flakes, salt, and pepper. Using a fork, break up the ground beef as much as possible. Cover the cooker and cook for 8 hours on "Low ."Serve and enjoy!
Nutrition: Cal 315; Fat 20g; Carbs 10g; Protein 21g

LETTUCE-WRAPPED BEEF ROAST

Preparation time: 5 minutes **Cooking time:** 8 hours 15 minutes
Serves 4
Ingredients:

- 2 lb beef chuck roast
- 8 romaine lettuce leaves
- 1 shallot, diced
- 1 cup beef broth
- 3 tbsp coconut aminos
- 1 tbsp rice vinegar
- 1 tsp garlic powder
- 1 tsp olive oil
- ½ tsp ground ginger
- ¼ tsp red pepper flakes
- 1 tbsp sesame seeds
- 1 scallion, diced

Direction:
Place the beef, shallot, broth, coconut aminos, vinegar, garlic powder, olive oil, ginger, and red pepper flakes in your slow cooker. Cover the oven and set it to "Low ."Cook for 8 hours. Scoop spoonfuls of the beef mixture into each lettuce leaf. Top with sesame seeds and scallion.
Nutrition: Cal 425; Fat 22g; Carbs 12g; Protein 45g

BEEF, TOMATO, AND LENTILS STEW

Preparation time: 10 minutes **Cooking time:** 10 minutes **Serves:**4
Ingredients:

- 1 pound extra-lean ground beef
- 1 can of lentils, drained
- 1 can chopped tomatoes with garlic and basil, drained
- 1 tablespoon extra-virgin olive oil
- 1 onion, chopped
- ½ teaspoon sea salt
- ⅛ teaspoon freshly ground black pepper

Directions:
Heat the olive oil in a pot over medium-high heat until shimmering.
Add the beef and onion to the pot and sauté for 5 minutes or until
the meat is lightly browned. Add the remaining ingredients. Bring to
a boil. Reduce the heat to medium and cook for 4 more minutes or
until the lentils are tender. Keep stirring during the cooking. Pour
them into a large serving bowl and serve immediately.
Nutrition: calories: 460 | fat: 14.8g | protein: 44.2g | carbs: 36.9g

BEEF KEBABS WITH ONION

Preparation time: 15 minutes **Cooking time:** 10 minutes **Serves:** 6
Ingredients:

- 2 pounds beef fillet
- 1 large onion, cut into 8 quarters
- 1 large red bell pepper, cut into 1-inch cubes
- 1½ teaspoons salt
- 1 teaspoon freshly ground black pepper
- ½ teaspoon ground nutmeg
- ½ teaspoon ground allspice
- ⅓ cup extra-virgin olive oil

Directions:
Preheat the grill to high heat. Cut the beef into 1-inch cubes and put them in a large bowl. Mix the salt, black pepper, allspice, and nutmeg in a small bowl. Pour the olive oil over the beef and toss to coat. Evenly sprinkle the seasoning over the meat and toss to coat all pieces. Skewer the beef, alternating every 1 or 2 pieces with a part of onion or bell pepper. To cook, place the skewers on the preheated grill, and flip every 2 to 3 minutes until all sides have cooked to desired doneness, 6 minutes for medium-rare, 8 minutes for well done. Serve hot.
Nutrition: calories: 485 | fat: 36.0g | protein: 35.0g | carbs: 4.0g

HERB PORK ROAST

Preparation Time: 10 minutes **Cooking Time:** 14 hours **Servings:** 10
Ingredients:

- 4 lbs. pork roast boneless or bone-in 1 tablespoon dry herb mix
- 4 garlic cloves cut into slivers
- 1 tablespoon salt

Directions:
Using a sharp knife, make minor cuts all over the meat, then insert garlic slivers into the cuts. Mix Italian herbs and salt in a small bowl and rub all over the pork roast. Place pork roast in the crock pot. Cover and cook on Low for 14 hours. Remove meat from the crock pot and shred using a fork. Serve and enjoy.
Nutrition: Calories 327 Fat 8 g Carbohydrates 0.5 g Sugar 0 g Protein 59 g Cholesterol 166 mg

POTATO LAMB AND OLIVE STEW

Preparation time: 20 minutes **Cooking time:** 3 hours 42 minutes
Serves: 10
Ingredients:

- 4 large shallots, cut into ½-inch wedges
- 1¼ pounds small potatoes halved
- 4 tablespoons almond flour
- ¾ cup low-sodium chicken stock
- 3 cloves garlic, minced
- 3 sprigs of fresh rosemary
- 1 tablespoon lemon zest
- Coarse sea salt and black pepper, to taste
- 3½ pounds lamb shanks, fat trimmed and cut crosswise into 1½- inch pieces
- 2 tablespoons extra-virgin olive oil
- ½ cup dry white wine
- 1 cup pitted green olives, halved
- 2 tablespoons lemon juice

Directions:
Combine 1 tablespoon of almond flour with chicken stock in a bowl. Stir to mix well. Put the flour mixture, potatoes, garlic, shallots, rosemary, and lemon zest in the slow cooker. Sprinkle with salt and black pepper. Stir to mix well. Set aside. Combine the remaining almond flour with salt and black pepper in a large bowl, dunk the lamb shanks in the flour and toss to coat. Heat the olive oil in a nonstick skillet over medium-high heat until shimmering. Add the

well-coated lamb and cook for 10 minutes or until golden brown. Flip the lamb pieces halfway through the cooking time. Transfer the cooked lamb to the slow cooker. Pour the wine into the same skillet, then cook for 2 minutes or until it reduces in half. Pour the wine into the slow cooker. Put the slow cooker lid on and cook on high for 3 hours and 30 minutes or until the lamb is very tender. In the last 20 minutes of the cooking, open the lid and fold in the olive halves to cook. Pour the stew onto a large plate, let them sit for 5 minutes, then skim any fat that remains over the face of the liquid. Drizzle with lemon juice and sprinkle with salt and pepper. Serve warm.

Nutrition: calories: 309 | fat: 10.3g | protein: 36.9g | carbs: 16.1g

BEEF, ARTICHOKE & MUSHROOM STEW

Preparation Time: 20 minutes **Cooking Time:** 2 hours and 15 minutes **Servings:** 6
Ingredients:

- 1½ pounds beef stew meat, cut into large chunks
- 1 onion, chopped
- 2 tablespoons tomato puree
- 1 garlic clove, crushed
- 12 ounces jar artichoke hearts, drained and cut into small chunks
- 2 tablespoons fresh thyme, hopped
- ½ cup dry red wine
- 2 tablespoons olive oil
- 1 teaspoon cayenne pepper
- Pinch of salt and ground black pepper
- 2 tablespoons all-purpose flour
- ½ cup water
- 4 ounces button mushrooms, sliced
- ½ cup dry red wine
- Salt and ground black pepper, as required
- 2 tablespoons olive oil

Directions:
In a large bowl, add all the except the beef and mix well. Add the meat and coat it with the marinade generously. Refrigerate to marinate overnight. Remove the beef from the bowl, reserving the

marinade. In a large pan, heat the oil and sear the beef in 2 batches for about 5 minutes or until browned. With a slotted spoon, transfer the beef into a bowl. Add the reserved marinade, flour, water, and wine to the same pan and stir to combine. Stir in the cooked beef and bring to a boil. Reduce the heat to low and simmer, covered for about 2 hours, stirring occasionally. Stir in the artichoke hearts and mushrooms and simmer for about 30 minutes. Stir in the salt and black pepper and bring to a boil over high heat. Remove from the heat ad serve hot.

Nutrition: Calories 367 Total Fat 16.6 g Saturated Fat 4 g Cholesterol 101mg Total Carbs 9.6 g Sugar 2.2 g Potassium 624 mg Protein 36.7

BEEF & TAPIOCA STEW

Preparation Time: 20 minutes **Cooking Time:** 1 hour and 45 minutes **Servings:** 8
Ingredients:

- 2 pounds boneless beef chuck roast, cut into
- 1 (14½-ounce) can of diced tomatoes with juice
- 2 cups beef broth
- 1 tablespoon olive oil
- 2 tbsp ground cinnamon
- ¾-inch cubes
- ¼ cup quick-cooking tapioca
- 3 cups sweet potato, peeled and cubed
- 2 medium onions, cut into thin wedges
- 1 tablespoon honey
- 2 cups prunes, pitted
- ¼ teaspoon garlic powder
- Ground black pepper, as required
- ¼ cup red wine vinegar

Directions:
In a Dutch oven, heat 1 tablespoon of oil over medium-high heat and sear the beef cubes in 2 batches for bout 4-5 minutes or until browned. Drain off the grease from the pan. Stir in the tomatoes, tapioca, honey, cinnamon, garlic powder, black pepper, vinegar, broth, and boil. Reduce the heat to low and simmer, covered for about 1 hour, stirring occasionally. Stir in the onions and sweet potato and simmer, coated, for about 20-30 minutes. Stir in the prunes and cook for about 3-5 minutes. Serve hot.

Nutrition: Calories 675 Cholesterol 117 mg Total Carbs 59.6 g
Sugar 26 mg Protein 34.1 g

PESTO PORK CHOPS

Preparation time: 20 minutes **Cooking time:** 20 minutes **Servings:** 4

Ingredients:

- 4 Pork top-loin chops
- 8 tsp Herb pesto
- ½ cup Breadcrumbs
- 1 Tbsp Olive oil

Directions:
Preheat the oven to 450°F. Line a baking sheet with foil. Set aside. Rub 1 tsp. Of pesto evenly over both sides of each pork chop. Lightly dredge each pork chop in the breadcrumbs. Heat the oil in a skillet. Brown the pork chops on each side for 5 minutes. Place the pork chops on the baking sheet. Bake for 10 minutes or until pork reaches 145°F in the center.

Nutrition: Calories: 210Kcal; Protein: 24g; Carbohydrates: 10g; Fat: 7g

GRILLED STEAK WITH SALSA

Preparation time: 20 minutes **Cooking time:** 15 minutes **Servings:** 4
Ingredients:
For the salsa

- 1 cup Chopped English cucumber
- ¼ cup Boiled and diced red bell pepper
- 1 Scallion, both green and white parts, chopped
- 2 Tbsps Chopped fresh cilantro
- Juice of 1 lime

For the steak

- 4 Beef tenderloin steaks, room temperature
- Olive oil
- Freshly ground black pepper

Directions:
In a bowl, to make, the salsa, combine the lime juice, cilantro, scallion, bell pepper, and cucumber. Set aside. To make the steak: Preheat a barbecue to medium heat.Rub the steaks all finished with oil and season with pepper. Grill the steaks for around 5 minutes each side for medium-rare, or until the desired doneness. Serve the steaks topped with salsa.
Nutrition: Calories: 130Kcal; Protein: 19g; Carbohydrates: 1g; Fat: 6g

BEEF WITH CARROT & BROCCOLI

Preparation time: 15 minutes **Cooking time:** 14 minutes **Servings:** 4

Ingredients:

- 2 tbsp. coconut oil, divided
- 2 medium garlic cloves, minced
- 1 lb. beef sirloin steak (sliced into thin strips)
- Salt, to taste
- ¼ cup chicken broth
- 2 tsp. fresh ginger, grated
- 1 tbsp. Ground flax seeds
- ½ tsp. Red pepper flakes, crushed
- ¼ tsp. freshly ground black pepper
- 1 large carrot, peeled and sliced thinly
- 2 cups broccoli florets
- 1 medium scallion, sliced thinly

Directions:

In a skillet, heat 1 tbsp. Of oil on medium-high heat. Put garlic and sauté approximately 1 minute. Add beef and salt and cook for at least 4-5 minutes or till browned. Using a slotted spoon, transfer the beef in a bowl. Take off the liquid from the skillet. In a bowl, put together broth, ginger, flax seeds, red pepper flakes, and black pepper then mix in the same skillet, heat remaining oil on medium heat. Put the carrot, broccoli, and ginger mixture then cook for at least 3-4 minutes or till desired doneness. Mix in beef and scallion then cook for around 3-4 minutes.

Nutrition: Calories: 412Kcal; Protein: 35g; Carbohydrates: 28g; Fat: 13g

OREGANO PORK

Preparation time: 10 minutes   **Cooking time:** 8 hours   **Servings:** 4

Ingredients:

- 2 pounds pork roast, sliced
- 2 tbsp. oregano, chopped
- ¼ cup balsamic vinegar
- 1 cup tomato paste
- 1 tbs. sweet paprika
- 1 tsp. onion powder
- 2 tbsp. chili powder
- 2 garlic cloves, minced
- A pinch of salt and black pepper

Directions:

In a slow cooker, combine the roast with the oregano, the vinegar, and the other ingredients, toss, put the lid on then cook on Low for 8 hours. Divide everything between plates and serve.

Nutrition: Calories: 300Kcal; Protein: 24g; Carbohydrates: 12g; Fat: 5g

CREAMY PORK AND TOMATOES

Preparation time: 10 minutes   **Cooking time:** 35 minutes   **Servings:** 4
Ingredients:

- 2 pounds pork stew meat, cubed
- 1 cup coconut cream
- 2 tbsp. avocado oil
- 1 cup tomatoes, cubed
- 1 tbs. mint, chopped
- 1 jalapeno pepper, chopped
- 1 tbs. hot pepper
- 2 tbsp. lemon juice
- Pinch of sea salt
- Pinch of black pepper

Directions:
Heat, a pan with the oil over medium heat, add the meat and brown for 5 minutes. Add the rest of the ingredients, toss, then cook over medium heat for 30 minutes more, divide between plates, and serve.
Nutrition: Calories: 230Kcal; Protein: 14g; Carbohydrates: 9g; Fat: 4g

PULLED PORK & CORIANDER WRAPS

Preparation time: 20 minutes **Cooking Time:** 4-5 Hours **Servings:** 8

Ingredients:

- 2 ½ lbs. boneless pork shoulder, trimmed of excess fat
- 16 corn tortillas
- ½ tsp. Himalayan salt
- 2 tbsp. all-purpose taco seasoning
- 2 tsp. extra-virgin avocado oil
- 2 cups chilled salsa (extra for serving)
- 1 lime, sliced into wedges
- ½ cup fresh coriander leaves, chopped

Directions:

Place the pork on a wooden chopping board, and slice the shoulder into 12 pieces roughly the same size. Sprinkle the meat with the salt and taco seasoning, and toss and massage the spices into the heart in an even layer. Place the seasoned pork in a large slow cooker, the avocado oil and 2 cups of salsa. Cook the pork on high for 4-5 hours or until it falls apart and can easily be shredded. Heat the corn wraps according to package instructions when the pork is cooked correctly. Once the pork has cooled slightly, place the meat on a chopping board, and shred it into fine pieces. Divide the shredded pork between the heated wraps, and top with extra salsa, a few squeezes of lime juice, fresh coriander leaves, and a few teaspoons of the slow cooker juices. Serve hot, and enjoy.

Nutrition: Calories: 250Kcal; Protein: 16g; Carbohydrates: 10g; Fat: 6g

BEEF BARBACOA BOWLS

Preparation Time: 30 Minutes **Cooking Time:** 10-11 Hours
Servings: 4
Ingredients:

- ¼ cup paleo mayonnaise
- ¼ cup beef stock
- 1 tbsp. sriracha sauce
- 2 tsp. freshly squeezed lime juice
- 2 tbsp. extra-virgin olive oil
- 2 lbs. chuck roast
- 1 tsp. Himalayan salt
- ½ tsp. white pepper
- 1 tsp. toasted sesame oil
- 1 tbsp. raw wild honey
- ½ cup coconut aminos
- 1 tbsp. fresh ginger, grated
- 3 tsp. crushed garlic
- 1 medium shallot, thinly sliced
- 2 tbsp. tapioca flour
- 4 cups basmati rice, cooked, for serving
- 1 cup kimchi
- 2 Hass avocados, peeled, pitted, and sliced
- ½ cup cucumbers, pitted and sliced
- 1 cup red onions, sliced
- Fresh coriander leaves, chopped, for garnish

- Spring onions, chopped, for garnish
- Toasted sesame seeds, for garnish

Directions:
Whisk together the mayonnaise, sriracha sauce, and lime juice in a small glass bowl. Seal the bowl with cling wrap, and chill for later. In a large frying pan over high heat, heat the oil. Place the chuck roast on a wooden chopping board and season with salt and pepper. When the oil is nice and hot, fry the chuck for 3-4 minutes per side, on all sides. Transfer the chuck to a large slow-cooker when all sides are correctly seared. Add the sesame oil, honey, coconut aminos, beef stock, ginger, garlic, and shallots to the slow cooker, stirring to combine. Cook on Low for 10 hours with the lid on the slow cooker. Use a sharp knife to shred the cooked beef. Spoon 2 tablespoons of the slow-cooker stock into a small bowl, and whisk in the tapioca flour. Add the mixture to the slow cooker and gently whisk the stock to combine. Turn the oven up to high, and cook with the lid on the pot for an additional 20 minutes or until the stock thickens. Divide the cooked rice between 4 serving bowls. Top the rice with layers of cooked beef, kimchi, avocados, cucumbers, and red onions. Garnish the bowls with coriander leaves, spring onions, and toasted sesame seeds. Place a dollop of the chilled mayo on each help and serve.

Nutrition: Calories: 330Kcal; Protein: 24g; Carbohydrates: 19g; Fat: 9g

HONEY-ROASTED CARROTS & CHOPS

Preparation time: 15-20 minutes **Cooking Time:** 45 Mins
Servings: 4
Ingredients:

- 12 lamb rib chops
- 1 ½ tsp. kosher salt
- 3 tbsp. fresh rosemary, finely chopped (divided)
- 1 tbsp. raw wild honey
- 2 tbsp. extra-virgin olive oil (divided)
- 1 lb. baby carrots
- ¼ tsp. garlic powder

Directions:
Cover a large, rimmed baking sheet with greaseproof paper, and set the oven to preheat to 400°F, with the wire rack 4-5 inches away from the broiler. Place a second wire rack in the center of the oven. Whisk together 1\2 teaspoon of salt, 1 tablespoon of rosemary, the honey, and 1 tablespoon of olive oil in a large bowl. Add the baby carrots, and toss until they are all evenly coated. Fan the coated carrots on the prepared baking sheet, pouring any extra sauce over them. Bake in the oven, on the middle rack, for 35-40 minutes or until the carrots are soft. Massage the remaining olive oil into the chops and season with the remaining salt, rosemary, and garlic powder. Lightly coat a baking tray with olive oil spray, and preheat the broiler. Arrange the seasoned chops on the tray, and broil in the oven for 4 minutes, flipping halfway through the cooking time. The chops should be cooked all the way through. Serve the lamb chops hot, with the baby carrots on the side.
Nutrition: Calories: 260Kcal; Protein: 15g; Carbohydrates: 9.8g; Fat: 4.8g

HEART SMART LAMB WRAPS

Preparation time: 5 minutes **Cooking Time:** 5-10 Mins Servings: 4
Ingredients:

- 12 oz. lean ground lamb
- 1 cup English cucumber, chopped
- 12 whole Boston lettuce leaves
- 1 cups shallots, finely chopped
- 1 tbsp. extra-virgin avocado oil
- 3 tsp. crushed garlic
- 1 tsp. ground cinnamon
- ¾ tsp. Himalayan salt
- ¼ tsp. white pepper
- 1 cup cherry tomatoes, quartered
- 3/4 cup refrigerated Greek yogurt tzatziki or cucumber-dill dip

Directions:

In a large frying pan over high heat, heat the avocado oil. When the oil is nice and hot, fry the garlic, shallots, lamb, cinnamon, salt, and pepper for about 5 minutes or until the lamb is cooked correctly. When the lamb is cooked, stir in the cucumber and tomatoes. Divide the lamb between the lettuce leaves, and top with tzatziki or dip before folding and serving.

Nutrition: Calories: 222Kcal; Protein: 13g; Carbohydrates: 9.3g; Fat: 4g

RICE PAPER ROLLS WITH BROCCOLI AND TOFU

Preparation time: 30 minutes **Cooking time:** 10 minutes **Serving:** 10

Ingredients:

- 10 rice paper wrappers
- 3 cups of broccoli
- 10 oz of Greek feta
- 5 dried cherry tomatoes
- 1 tablespoon of sesame seeds
- 2 tablespoons of black olive pate
- 1 tablespoon of olive oil
- a pinch of salt

Directions:

In a pot of lightly salted boiling water, cook the broccoli for about 10 minutes, drain very well, and put them in a bowl. Chop the dried tomatoes to the broccoli, then add the salt, pepper, sesame seeds, olive pate, and coarsely crumbled feta. Mix everything with a fork. Wet a rice waffle by immersing it in a bowl of cold water for a few moments. Place it on the work surface and stuff it in the center with the vegetables, then wrap the rice paper on itself. Repeat the process with all the rolls. Arrange the rice paper wrappers on a serving tray and serve.

Nutrition: calories: 135 / fat: 9 / protein: 5 / carbs: 10 /

SPINACH WITH CHICKPEAS AND LEMON

Preparation Time: 10 minutes **Cooking Time:** 15 minutes
Servings: 2
Ingredients:

- 3 tbsp extra virgin olive oil
- Sea salt, to taste
- ½ container of grape tomatoes
- 1 large can of chickpeas, rinse well
- 1 large onion, thinly sliced
- 1 tbsp ginger, grated
- 1 large lemon, zested and freshly juiced
- 1 tsp red pepper flakes, crushed
- 4 garlic cloves, minced

Directions
Pour the olive oil into a large skillet and add the onion. Cook for about 5 minutes until the onion starts to brown. Add in the ginger, lemon zest, garlic, tomatoes, and red pepper flakes, and cook for 3–4 minutes. Toss in the chickpeas (rinsed and drained) and cook for 3–4 minutes. Now add the spinach in 2 batches, and once it starts to wilt, season with sea salt and lemon juice. Cook for 2 minutes.
Nutrition Calories: 312 Kcal; Protein: 28 g; Carbohydrates: 80 g; Fat: 9 g

ZUCCHINI FRITTERS WITH GARLIC SAUCE

Preparation time: 30 minutes **Cooking time:** 15 minutes **Serving:** 4
Ingredients:

- 5 courgettes
- 2 eggs
- 3 tablespoons of rice flour
- 2 tablespoons of nutritional yeast
- 1 cup unsweetened coconut yogurt
- 3 tablespoons of grated quinoa bread (see recipe)
- 8 fresh mint leaves
- 2 cloves of garlic
- 3 tablespoons of olive oil
- 1 pinch of black pepper
- 1 pinch of salt

Directions:
Put the yogurt in a colander with a bowl and put it in the refrigerator for 30 minutes. After this time, the yogurt will have eliminated the excess water; season it with a pinch of salt and minced garlic and put it back in the refrigerator. Wash the courgettes and cut them into julienne strips, beat the eggs, and add them to the courgettes, breadcrumbs, nutritional yeast, salt and pepper, and chopped mint. In a non-stick pan, lightly heat the olive oil and cook the pancakes by spoonfuls, turning them brown on both sides. Serve the fritters hot with the coconut sauce.
Nutrition: calories: 238 / fat: 16 / protein: 7 / carbs: 13

CARROT PATTIES

Preparation time: 5 minutes **Cooking time**: 5 minutes **Servings:** 4
Ingredients:

- 1 lb carrots, grated
- 1 clove garlic, minimum
- 4 eggs
- ¼ cups of all-purpose flour
- ¼ cups of bread crumbs or matzo meal
- ½ tsp. salt
- 1 pinch of ground black pepper
- 2 tbsp. vegetable oil

Directions:
Grated carrots, garlic, eggs, flour, bread crumbs, salt, and black pepper should all be combined in a medium-sized mixing basin and thoroughly mixed. In a frying pan, heat the oil over medium-high heat. Create patties from the ingredients, then cook them in hot oil until all sides are browned.

Nutrition: 236 cals; protein 9.1g; carbs 22.5g; fat 12.6g; chole 186mg; sodium 488.8mg.

SWEET POTATO QUINOA BOWL

Preparation Time: 15 minutes **Cooking Time:** 20 minutes
Servings: 1
Ingredients:

- 1 medium sweet potato, cubed
- Extra-virgin olive oil for drizzling
- ¼ cup almonds, toasted and chopped
- 2 cups baby salad greens
- Juice of ½ lemon, more to taste
- Sea salt and freshly ground black pepper
- ½ cup cooked chickpeas, drained and rinsed
- 1 cup cooked quinoa
- 2 scallions, finely chopped
- ¼ cup thinly sliced red cabbage
- ⅓ cup crumbled feta cheese

Directions:
Preheat the oven to 400° F. and prepare a baking sheet with parchment paper. Toss the sweet potatoes with a drizzle of olive oil and salt and pepper to taste. Roast for 25 to 35 minutes or until golden brown. In a large mixing bowl, combine the roasted sweet potatoes, chickpeas, quinoa, scallions, cabbage, feta, almonds, and salad leaves. Drizzle with olive oil, lemon juice, and pinches of salt and pepper to taste. Season with extra lemon juice to taste. Toss everything together and serve in bowls.
Nutrition: 373 cals; protein 18.3g; carbs 57.9g; fat 9.2g; sodium 584.8mg.

PESTO AVOCADO

Preparation Time: 10 minutes **Cooking Time:** 10 minutes
Servings: 2
Ingredients

- 1 avocado pitted, halved
- ⅓ cup Mozzarella balls, cherry size
- 1 cup fresh basil
- 1 tbsp walnut
- ¼ tsp garlic, minced
- ¾ tsp salt
- ¾ tsp black pepper, ground
- 4 tbsp olive oil
- 1 oz. Parmesan, grated
- ⅓ cup cherry tomatoes

Directions
Make pesto sauce: blend salt, minced garlic, walnuts, fresh basil, ground black pepper, and olive oil. When the mixture is smooth, augment the grated cheese and pulse it for 3 seconds more. Then scoop ½ flesh from the avocado halves. In the mixing bowl, mix up together mozzarella balls and cherry tomatoes. Add pesto sauce and shake it well. Preheat the oven to 360°F. Fill the avocado halves with the cherry tomato mixture and bake for 10 minutes.
Nutrition Calories: 421 Kcal; Protein: 8.2 g; Carbohydrates: 11.7 g; Fat: 43 g

GUACAMOLE

Preparation Time: 15 minutes **Cooking Time:** 20 minutes
Servings: 1
Ingredients:

- 1 jalapeno pepper finely diced
- 3 avocados, ripe
- 2 garlic cloves, minced
- 1 lime, juiced
- 1/2 teaspoon sea salt
- 1/2 small onion, finely diced
- 2 Roma tomatoes, diced
- 3 tablespoons finely chopped fresh cilantro

Directions:

With a fork, mash the avocado until it's as chunky or smooth as you desire. Combine the remaining ingredients in a mixing bowl. Taste it and adjust it with extra salt or lime juice if necessary. Guacamole should be served with tortilla chips.

Nutrition: 382 cals; protein 19.3g; carbs 56.9g; fat 9.2g; sodium 561.8mg.

STUFFED PORTOBELLO MUSHROOMS WITH SPINACH

Preparation time: 5 minutes **Cooking time:** 20 minutes **Serves:** 4
Ingredients:

- 8 large portobello mushrooms, stems removed
- 3 teaspoons extra-virgin olive oil, divided
- 1 medium red bell pepper, diced
- 4 cups fresh spinach
- ¼ cup crumbled feta cheese

Directions:
Preheat the oven to 450°F. Using a spoon to scoop out the gills of the mushrooms and discard them. Brush the mushrooms with 2 teaspoons of olive oil. Arrange the mushrooms (cap-side down) on a baking sheet. Roast in the preheated oven for 20 minutes. In a medium skillet, heat the remaining olive oil over medium heat until it shimmers. Add the bell pepper and spinach and saute for 8 to 10 minutes, stirring occasionally, or until the spinach is wilted. Remove the mushrooms from the oven to a paper towel-lined plate. Using a spoon, stuff each mushroom with the bell pepper and spinach mixture. Scatter the feta cheese all over. Serve immediately.
Nutrition: calories: 115 | fat: 5.9g | protein: 7.2g | carbs: 11.5g

CHICKPEA LETTUCE WRAPS WITH CELERY

Preparation time: 10 minutes **Cooking time:** 0 minutes **Serves:** 4
Ingredients:

- 1 (15-ounce / 425-g) can of low-sodium chickpeas, drained and rinsed
- 1 celery stalk, thinly sliced
- 2 tablespoons finely chopped red onion
- 2 tablespoons unsalted tahini
- 3 tablespoons honey mustard
- 1 tablespoon capers, undrained
- 12 butter lettuce leaves

Directions:
In a bowl, mash the chickpeas with a potato masher or the back of a fork until mostly smooth. Add the celery, red onion, tahini, honey mustard, and capers to the bowl and stir until well incorporated. For each serving, place three overlapping lettuce leaves on a plate and top with ¼ of the mashed chickpea filling, then roll up. Repeat with the remaining lettuce leaves and chickpea mixture.
Nutrition: calories: 182 | fat: 7.1g | protein: 10.3g | carbs: 19.6g

ZOODLES WITH WALNUT PESTO

Preparation time: 10 minutes **Cooking time:** 10 minutes **Serves:** 4
Ingredients:

- 4 medium zucchinis, spiralized
- ¼ cup extra-virgin olive oil, divided
- 1 teaspoon minced garlic, divided
- ½ teaspoon crushed red pepper
- ¼ teaspoon freshly ground black pepper, divided
- ¼ teaspoon kosher salt, divided
- 2 tablespoons grated Parmesan cheese, divided
- 1 cup packed fresh basil leaves
- ¾ cup walnut pieces divided

Directions:

In a large bowl, stir together the zoodles, 1 tablespoon of olive oil, ½ teaspoon of minced garlic, red pepper, ⅛ teaspoon of black pepper, and ⅛ teaspoon of salt. Set aside. Heat ½ tablespoon of the oil in a large skillet over medium-high heat. Add half of the zoodles to the skillet and cook for 5 minutes, stirring constantly. Transfer the cooked zoodles to a bowl. Repeat with another ½ tablespoon of the oil and the remaining zoodles. When done, add the cooked zoodles to the bowl.

Make the pesto:

In a food processor, combine the remaining ½ teaspoon of minced garlic, ⅛ teaspoon of black pepper and ⅛ teaspoon of salt, 1 tablespoon of Parmesan, basil leaves, and ¼ cup of walnuts. Pulse until smooth, then slowly drizzle the remaining 2 tablespoons of the oil into the pesto. Pulse again until well combined. Add the pesto to

the zoodles, the remaining 1 tablespoon of Parmesan, and the remaining ½ cup of walnuts. Toss to coat well. Serve immediately.
Nutrition: calories: 166 | fat: 16.0g | protein: 4.0g | carbs: 3.0g

SPICY MUSHROOM STIR-FRY

Preparation Time: 15 minutes **Cooking Time:** 10 minutes
Servings: 4
Ingredients

- 1 cup low-sodium vegetable broth
- 2 tbsp cornstarch
- 1 tsp low-sodium soy sauce
- ½ tsp ginger, ground
- ⅛ tsp cayenne pepper
- 2 tbsp olive oil
- 2 (8-oz.) packages of button mushrooms, sliced
- 1 red bell pepper, chopped
- 1 jalapeño pepper, minced
- 3 cups of brown rice that has been cooked in unsalted water
- 2 tbsp sesame oil

Directions
Whisk together the broth, cornstarch, soy sauce, ginger, and cayenne pepper in a mini bowl and set aside. Warm the olive oil in a wok or heavy skillet over high heat. Add the mushrooms, peppers, and stir-fry for 3 to 5 minutes or until the vegetables are tender-crisp. Stir the broth mixture and add it to the wok; stir-fry for 3 to 5 minutes longer or until the vegetables are tender and the sauce has thickened. Serve the stir-fry over the hot cooked brown rice and drizzle with the sesame oil.
Nutrition: Calories: 916 Kcal; Protein: 19 g; Carbohydrates: 122 g; Fat: 38 g

SPICY VEGGIE PANCAKES

Preparation Time: 20 minutes **Cooking Time:** 10 minutes
Servings: 4
Ingredients:

- 3 tbsp olive oil, divided
- 2 small onions, finely chopped
- 1 jalapeño pepper, minced
- ¾ cup carrot, grated
- ¾ cup cabbage, finely chopped
- 1½ cups quick-cooking oats
- ¾ cup brown rice, cooked
- ¾ cup of water
- ½ cup whole-wheat flour
- 1 large egg
- 1 large egg white
- 1 tsp baking soda
- ¼ tsp cayenne pepper

Directions:
Warm 2 tsp oil in a medium skillet over medium temperature. Sauté the onion, jalapeño, carrot, and cabbage for 4 minutes. While the vegetables are cooking, combine the oats, rice, water, flour, egg white, cayenne pepper, and baking soda in a medium bowl until well mixed. Add the cooked vegetables to the mixture and stir to combine. Heat the remaining oil in a large skillet over medium heat. Drop the mixture into the skillet, about ⅓ cup per pancake. Cook for 4 minutes until bubbles form on the pancakes' surface, and the edges look cooked, then carefully flip them over. Cook the other

side for 3 to 5 minutes until the pancakes are hot and firm. Repeat with the remaining mixture and serve.
Nutrition Calories: 619 Kcal; Protein: 26 g; Carbohydrates: 73 g; Fat: 25 g

EGG AND VEGGIE FAJITAS

Preparation Time: 20 minutes **Cooking Time:** 10 minutes
Servings: 4
Ingredients

- 3 large eggs
- 3 egg whites
- 2 tsp chili powder
- 1 tbsp butter, unsalted
- 1 onion, chopped
- 2 garlic cloves, minced
- 1 jalapeño pepper, minced
- 1 red bell pepper, chopped
- 1 cup corn, frozen, thawed and drained
- 8 (6") corn tortillas

Directions:
Whisk the eggs, egg whites, and chili powder in a small bowl until well combined. Set aside. In a large skillet, dissolve the butter at medium temperature. Sauté the onion, garlic, jalapeño, bell pepper, and corn until the vegetables are tender, 3 to 4 minutes. Put the beaten egg mixture into the skillet. Cook, occasionally stirring, until the eggs form large curds and are set, 3 to 5 minutes. Meanwhile, soften the corn tortillas as directed on the package. Divide the egg mixture evenly among the softened corn tortillas. Roll the tortillas up and serve.
Nutrition: Calories: 891 Kcal; Protein: 43 g; Carbohydrates: 111 g; Fat: 32 g

CHAPTER 13: SNACK

DIJON ROASTED ASPARAGUS

Preparation time: 5 minutes **Cooking time:** 35 minutes **Serves** 4
Ingredients:

- 2 tbsp extra-virgin olive oil
- 1 lb asparagus, trimmed
- 2 garlic cloves, minced
- 1 tsp Dijon mustard
- 1 tbsp lemon juice

Direction:

Warm the olive oil in a large skillet and sauté the asparagus until softened with some crunch, 7 minutes. Mix in the garlic and cook until fragrant, 30 seconds. Whisk the mustard and lemon juice in a small bowl and pour the mixture over the asparagus. Cook for 2 minutes. Plate the asparagus. Serve warm.

Nutrition: Cal 90; Fat 7g; Carbs 5g; Protein 3g

PAPRIKA TOFU & ZUCCHINI SKEWERS

Preparation time: 5 minutes **Cooking time:** 10 minutes **Serves** 4
Ingredients:

- 1 (14 oz) block tofu, cubed
- 1 zucchini, cut into rounds
- 2 tbsp lemon juice
- 1 tsp smoked paprika
- 1 tbsp extra-virgin olive oil
- 1 tsp cumin powder
- 1 tsp garlic powder
- Sea salt and pepper to taste

Direction:
Preheat a grill to medium heat. Meanwhile, thread the tofu and zucchini alternately on the wooden skewers. Whisk the olive oil, lemon juice, paprika, cumin powder, and garlic powder in a small bowl. Brush the skewers with the mixture and place them on the grill grate. Cook on both sides until golden brown, 5 minutes. Season with salt and pepper and serve afterward.
Nutrition: Cal 115; Fat 8g; Carbs 5g; Protein 8g

CHOCOLATE BARS WITH WALNUTS

Preparation time: 5 minutes **Cooking time:** 60 minutes **Serves** 4
Ingredients:

- 1 cup walnuts
- 3 tbsp sunflower seeds
- 2 tbsp dark chocolate chips
- 1 tbsp cocoa powder
- 1 ½ tsp vanilla extract
- ¼ tsp cinnamon powder
- 2 tbsp melted coconut oil
- 2 tbsp toasted almond meal
- 2 tsp pure maple syrup

Direction:
In a food processor, add the walnuts, sunflower seeds, chocolate chips, cocoa powder, vanilla extract, cinnamon powder, coconut oil, almond meal, and maple syrup, and blitz a few times until combined. Line a flat baking sheet with plastic wrap, pour the mixture onto the sheet and place another plastic wrap on top. Use a rolling pin to flatten the batter and remove the top plastic wrap. Freeze the snack until firm, 1 hour. Remove from the freezer, cut into 1 ½-inch bar, and enjoy immediately.
Nutrition: Cal 300; Fat 26g; Carbs 20g; Protein 5g

APPLE AND CINNAMON CHIPS

Preparation time: 20 minutes **Cooking time:** 120 minutes **Serving:** 2

Ingredients:

- 2 apples
- 1 teaspoon ground cinnamon
- 1 teaspoon of vanilla powder
- 1 teaspoon of ghee
- 2 limes

Directions:

Squeeze the limes, then stir in the cinnamon, ghee, and vanilla powder. Peel the apples and cut them into skinny slices. Preheat the oven to 200°F. Grease the apples on both sides with a kitchen brush and place them on a baking sheet lined with parchment paper. Cook for two hours, monitoring it often.

Nutrition: calories: 158 / fat: 3 / protein: 2 / carbs: 36 /

CELERY WITH CURRY SAUCE

Preparation time: 15 minutes **Cooking time:** 0 minutes **Serving:** 3
Ingredients:

- 1 celery
- 1 cup unsweetened soy yogurt
- 1 teaspoon of curry
- 1 pinch of salt
- 1 teaspoon of fennel seeds

Directions:
Wash and chop the celery into little sticks. Combine the soy yogurt, curry, salt, and crushed fennel seeds using a pestle. Put the celery sticks on a platter and the sauce in shot glasses.

Nutrition: calories: 60 / fat: 1 / protein: 3 / carbs: 8 /

SKEWERS OF TOFU AND ZUCCHINI

Preparation time: 5 minutes **Cooking time:** 5 minutes **Serving:** 6
Ingredients:

- 7 oz. of smoked tofu
- 2 courgettes
- 2 tablespoons of olive oil
- 1 pinch of salt
- 1 pinch of red pepper

Directions:
Brown the tofu cubes in a nonstick skillet with a tablespoon of oil for 5 minutes. Cut the courgettes into slices and brush them with the fat previously combined with the salt and chile pepper. Cook the courgettes without allowing them to burn. Repeat with a cube of tofu and a slice of courgette on a skewer with a toothpick. Continue until all of the ingredients have been eaten.
Nutrition: calories: 127 / fat: 9 / protein: 8 / carbs: 4 /

CRISPS MADE FROM SWEET POTATO

Preparation time: 20 minutes **Cooking time:** 2 hours **Servings:** 4 to 6

Ingredients:

- 2 sweet potatoes,
- 3 tablespoons extra-virgin olive oil
- 1 teaspoon sea salt

Direction:
Preheat the oven to 250°Fahrenheit. Place the rack in the oven to be centered in the range. Pour the olive oil over the sliced sweet potatoes in a large basin and toss to combine. Arrange the slices so that they are in a single layer on both of the baking sheets. The sea salt should be sprinkled on top. Place the baking sheets in a prepared oven and bake for about 2 hours, turning the chips and rotating the pans after the first hour has passed. Take the chips out of the range after achieving the desired browning and crispiness level. Some of them could be a bit mushy, but they will crisp up as they cool. Before serving, let the chips cool down for ten minutes. Serve as soon as possible. After sitting out for a few hours, the chips have lost their crunch.

Nutrition: Calories; 267 fat; 11 g carbohydrates; 42 g sugar;1 g fiber;6 g protein;2 g sodium;482 mg

STICKS WITH SESAME AND TURMERIC

Preparation time: 5 minutes **Cooking time:** 10 minutes **Serving:** 10

Ingredients:

- 1 cup of almond flour
- 1 tsp of sesame seeds
- 2 egg whites
- 1 pinch of salt
- 1 pinch of pepper
- 1 teaspoon of turmeric

Directions:

Mix the flour with the salt, pepper, and turmeric. Add the sesame seeds and mix again. Beat the egg whites and mix well. Line a baking sheet with parchment paper, divide the dough into 10, and form cylinders with your hands. Cook at 350° F for about 10 minutes.

Nutrition: calories: 91 / fat: 7 / protein: 4 / carbs: 3 /

QUINOA AND LEMON COOKIES

Preparation time: 20 minutes **Cooking time:** 25 minutes **Serving:** 10

Ingredients:

- 2 ½ cups of wholemeal flour
- 1 ½ cups of quinoa flour
- 5 tablespoons of ghee
- 1 organic lemon
- 4 tablespoons of maple syrup
- 1 teaspoon of cardamom powder
- 1 pinch of salt

Directions:

Cook the quinoa in a pot of unsalted boiling water for about 15 minutes, drain well and let it cool. Mix the two flours with the salt and cardamom. Grate the lemon zest and add it to the flour. Mix. Combine lemon juice, maple syrup, and ghee and knead. If the dough is too dry, add a few tablespoons of vegetable milk. Roll out the dough and form discs. Line a baking sheet, arrange the discs, and bake at 350° F for about 10 minutes.

Nutrition: calories: 241 / fat: 5 / protein: 8 / carbs: 42 /

APPLE AND CINNAMON CHIPS

Preparation time: 20 minutes **Cooking time:** 120 minutes **Serving:** 2

Ingredients:

- 2 apples
- 1 teaspoon ground cinnamon
- 1 teaspoon of vanilla powder
- 1 teaspoon of ghee
- 2 limes

Directions:

Squeeze the limes, add the cinnamon, ghee, and vanilla powder to the juice and mix well. Peel the apples into skinny slices. Heat the oven to 200° F. With the help of a kitchen brush, grease the apples on both sides and spread them on a baking sheet lined with baking paper. Cook for about two hours, checking often.

Nutrition: calories: 158 / fat: 3 / protein: 2 / carbs: 36

CHOCOLATE BEET CAKE

Preparation time:10 minutes **Cooking time:**50 minutes
Servings:12
Ingredients:

- 3 cups of grated beets
- 1/4 cup of canola oil
- 4 eggs
- 4 oz. of unsweetened chocolate
- 2 tsp. of Phosphorus-free baking powder
- 2 cups of all-purpose flour
- 1 cup of sugar

Directions:
Set your oven to 325°F. Grease two 8-inch cake pans. Mix the baking powder, flour, and sugar. Set aside. Slice up the chocolate as excellently as you can and melt using a double boiler. A microwave can also be used, but don't let it burn. Allow it to cool, and then mix in the oil and eggs. Mix all of the wet ingredients into the flour mixture and combine everything until well mixed. Fold the beets in and pour the batter into the cake pans. Let them bake for 40 to 50 minutes. To know it's done, the toothpick should come out clean when inserted into the cake. Remove from the oven and allow them to cool. Once cool, invert over a plate to remove. It is great when served with whipped cream and fresh berries. Enjoy!
Nutrition: Calories: 270Kcal; Protein: 6g; Carbohydrates: 21g; Fat: 6g

STRAWBERRY PIE

Preparation time: 25 minutes **Cooking time:** 3 hours **Servings:** 8
Ingredients:
For the Crust:

- 1 1/2 cups of Graham cracker crumbs
- 5 tbsp. of unsalted butter
- 2 tbsp. of sugar

For the Pie:

- 1 1/2 tsp. of gelatin powder
- 3 tbsp. of cornstarch
- 3/4 cup of sugar
- 5 cups of sliced strawberries, divided
- 1 cup of water

Directions:
For the crust:
Heat your oven to 375°F. Grease a pie pan. Combine the butter, crumbs, and sugar, and then press them into your pie pan. Bake the crust for around 10 to 15 minutes, until lightly browned. Take out of the oven and let it cool completely.
For the pie:
Crush up a cup of strawberries. Using a small pot, combine the sugar, water, gelatin, and cornstarch. Bring the mixture in the pot up to a boil, lower the heat, and simmer until it has thickened. Add in the crushed strawberries in the pot and let it simmer for another 5 minutes until the sauce has thickened up again. Set it off the heat and pour it into a bowl. Cool until it comes to room temperature. Toss the remaining berries with the sauce to be well distributed, pour

into the pie crust, and spread it into an even layer. Refrigerate the pie until cold. It will take about 3 hours. Serve and enjoy!
Nutrition: Calories: 265Kcal; Protein: 3g; Carbohydrates: 10g; Fat: 8g

GRAPE SKILLET GALETTE

Preparation time: 20 minutes **Cooking time:** 2 hours **Servings:**6
Ingredients:
For the Crust:

- 1/2 cup of unsweetened rice milk
- 4 tbsp. of cold butter
- 1 tbsp. of sugar
- 1 cup of all-purpose flour

For the Galette:

- 1 tbsp. of cornstarch
- 1/3 cup of sugar
- One egg white
- 2 cups of halved seedless grapes

Directions:
For the crust:
Add the sugar and the flour to a food processor and mix for a few seconds. Place in the butter and pulse until it looks like a coarse meal. Add in the rice milk and combine until the dough forms. Put the dough on a clean surface and form it into a disc. Wrap it with plastic wrap and place it in the fridge for 2 hours.
For the galette:
Set your oven to 425°F. Mix the cornstarch and sugar and toss the grapes in. Unwrap the dough and roll it out on a floured surface. Press it into a 14-inch circle and place it in a cast-iron skillet. Add the grape filling in the center and spread out to fill, leaving a 2-inch crust. Fold the edge over. Brush the crust with egg white and cook

for 20 to 25 minutes. The crust should be golden. Allow to rest for around 20 minutes before you serve. Enjoy!

Nutrition: Calories: 172Kcal; Protein: 2g; Carbohydrates: 8g; Fat: 3g

TAPIOCA PUDDING

Preparation time: 5 minutes **Cooking time:** 20 minutes **Servings:** 6

Ingredients:

- 2 C. low-fat milk
- 2 tbsp. quick-cooking tapioca
- 2 eggs, lightly beaten
- ⅓ C. sugar
- ½ tsp. vanilla
- 1 C. water

Directions:
Heat the milk and tapioca. Remove from heat then let stand 15 minutes. Combine eggs, sugar, and vanilla. Add milk and tapioca, stirring constantly. Pour them into individual cups for custard. Cover each cup firmly with the foil. Pour the water into the pot. Position the cups on the rack of the pot. Close and secure the lid. Place the pressure regulator on the vent tube and cook for 5 minutes once the pressure regulator begins to rock slowly. Excellent the pot quickly. Let the pudding cool well in the refrigerator.
Nutrition: Calories: 113Kcal; Protein:12g; Carbohydrates: 21g; Fat: 8g

MANGO MUG CAKE

Preparation time: 5 minutes **Cooking time**: 10 minutes
Servings: 2
Ingredients:

- 1 medium-sized mango, peeled and diced
- 2 eggs
- 1 tsp. Vanilla
- ¼ tsp. nutmeg, grated
- 1 tbsp. cocoa powder
- 2 tbsp. honey
- ½ C. coconut flour

Directions:
Combine the coconut flour, eggs, honey, vanilla, nutmeg, and cocoa powder in 2 lightly greased mugs. Then, add 1 C. of water and a metal trivet to the Instant Pot. Lower the uncovered mugs onto the trivet. Secure the lid. Choose the "Manual" mode and High pressure; cook for 10 minutes. Once cooking is complete, use a quick pressure release; carefully remove the lid. Top with diced mango and serve chilled. Enjoy!
Nutrition: Calories: 268Kcal; Protein: 10g; Carbohydrates:34g; Fat: 10g

HONEY STEWED APPLES

Preparation time: 5 minutes **Cooking time:** 5 minutes **Servings:** 4
Ingredients:

- 2 tbsp. honey
- 1 tsp. Cinnamon, ground
- ½ tsp. cloves, ground
- 4 apples

Directions:
Add all ingredients to the inner pot. Now, pour in ⅓ C. of water. Secure the lid. Choose the "Manual" mode and cook for 2 minutes at high pressure. Once cooking is complete, use a quick pressure release; carefully remove the lid. Serve in individual bowls. Bon appétit!
Nutrition: Calories: 128Kcal; Protein: 0g; Carbohydrates:34g; Fat: 0g

APRICOT CAKE

Preparation time: 15 minutes **Cooking time:** 25 minutes **Servings:** 8

Ingredients:

- 1 ½ cups of wholemeal flour
- 1 ½ cups of almond flour
- 3/4 cup of rice milk
- 1 teaspoon of salt
- 1 tablespoon of chopped pecans
- 1 tablespoon of chopped hazelnuts
- 4 dried apricots cut into small pieces
- 4 tablespoons of almond butter

Directions:
Mix the two flours with the almond butter, the water, the milk, and the salt, mix well and let the dough rest in a cling film for about half an hour. After this time, roll out the dough, put the pecans, hazelnuts and apricots in the center, and knead again. Leave to rest for 10 minutes. Roll out the dough into a lightly greased ovenproof dish and bake in a hot oven at 350° F for about 25 minutes.

Nutrition: Calories: 325kcal; Fat: 20g; Protein: 10g; Carbs: 25g

PUMPKIN AND DATES CAKE

Preparation time: 15 minutes **Cooking time:** 20 minutes **Servings:** 8

Ingredients:

- ¾ cup of wholemeal flour
- ¼ cup of almond flour
- 4 cups boiled cubed squash
- 4 apples, peeled and cut into wedges
- 4 pitted dates
- 1 teaspoon of coconut butter

Directions:

Mix the flours. Put the pumpkin and dates in the blender and blend. Mix the flour with the date and pumpkin cream. Grease a pan, pour in the mixture, and decorate with the sliced apples standing in the dough. Bake at 400° F for about 20 minutes.

Nutrition: Calories: 170kcal; Fat: 4g; Protein: 4g; Carbs: 32g

MINT CHOCOLATES

Preparation time: 15 minutes **Cooking time:** 0 minutes **Servings:** 20

Ingredients:

- 1 cup of dried and grated coconut
- ½ cup of almond flour
- 1 teaspoon of maple syrup
- 1 teaspoon of raw honey
- ½ cup of coconut oil
- 5 oz. of ghee
- 2 tablespoons of 70% dark cocoa powder
- 2 tablespoons of powdered mint extract

Directions:

Mix and blend all the ingredients in the blender. Pour the cream into chocolate molds and refrigerate for three hours.

Nutrition: Calories: 186kcal; Fat: 16g; Protein: 2g; Carbs: 4g

PEANUT BUTTER AND CHOCOLATE BALLS

Preparation time: 45 minutes **Cooking time:** 0 mins **Serves:**15 balls
Ingredients:

- ¾ cup creamy peanut butter
- ¼ cup unsweetened cocoa powder
- 2 tablespoons softened almond butter
- ½ teaspoon vanilla extract
- 1¾ cups maple syrup

Directions:
Line a baking sheet with parchment paper. Combine all the ingredients in a bowl. Stir to mix well. Divide the mixture into 15 parts and shape each portion into a 1-inch ball. Arrange the balls on the baking sheet and refrigerate for at least 30 minutes, then serve chilled.
Nutrition: calories: 146 | fat: 8.1g | protein: 4.2g | carbs: 16.9g

SPICED SWEET PECANS

Preparation time: 4 minutes **Cooking time:** 17 minutes **Serves:** 4
Ingredients:

- 1 cup pecan halves
- 3 tablespoons almond butter
- 1 teaspoon ground cinnamon
- ½ teaspoon ground nutmeg
- ¼ cup raw honey
- ¼ teaspoon sea salt

Directions:
Preheat the oven to 350°F. Line a baking sheet with parchment paper. Combine all the ingredients in a bowl. Stir to mix well, then spread the mixture in a single layer on the baking sheet with a spatula. Bake in the oven for 16 minutes or until the pecan halves are well browned. Serve immediately.
Nutrition: calories: 324 | protein: 3.2g | carbs: 13.9g

GREEK YOGURT AFFOGATO WITH PISTACHIOS

Preparation time: 5 minutes **Cooking time:** 0 minutes **Serves:** 4
Ingredients:

- 24 ounces vanilla Greek yogurt
- 2 teaspoons sugar
- 4 shots of hot espresso
- 4 tablespoons chopped unsalted pistachios
- 4 tablespoons dark chocolate chips

Directions:
Spoon the yogurt into four bowls or tall glasses. Mix ½ teaspoon of sugar into each of the espresso shots. Pour one shot of the hot espresso over each bowl of yogurt. Top each bowl with 1 tablespoon of the pistachios and 1 tablespoon of the chocolate chips, and serve.
Nutrition: calories: 190 | fat: 6.0g | protein: 20.0g | carbs: 14.0g

DESSERT CREPES

Preparation time: 10-minute **Cooking time:** 20 minutes **Servings:** 8

Ingredients:

- 4 eggs, lightly beaten
- 1 ⅓ cups of milk
- 1 cup of all-purpose flour
- 2 tbsp. butter, melted
- 2 tbsp. White sugar
- ½ tsp. salt

Directions:

In a big bowl, stir the eggs, milk, flour, melted butter, sugar, and salt until everything is well combined. Over medium heat, preheat a medium skillet or crepe pan. Use a paper towel or a little oil or butter to grease the pan lightly. About 3 tbsp. Crepe batter should be poured onto the hot skillet using a serving spoon or small ladle. Tilt the pan to coat the bottom surface evenly. Serve heated after cooking for 1 to 2 minutes per side until golden brown.

Nutrition: 164 cals; protein 6.4g; carbs 17.2g; fat 7.7g; chole 111.1mg; sodium 234.5mg.

LEMON PINEAPPLE DESSERT

Preparation time: 5-minute **Cooking time:** 30 minutes. **Servings:** 4

Ingredients:

- 1 (6 Oz.) c nonfat vanilla yogurt
- 1 (6 Oz.) c nonfat lemon yogurt
- 1 (8 Oz.) can of crushed pineapple, drained
- 1 (3 Oz.) package of fat-free, sugar-free lemon pudding mix
- 1 cup of low-fat frozen whipped topping thawed
- 4 tsp. toasted coconut
- 4 fresh blueberries

Directions

Mix the pudding, pineapple, vanilla, and lemon yogurt in a bowl, and whisk to blend thoroughly. Whip the topping in. The mixture should be divided among 4 dessert dishes, then chilled for around 30 minutes. If you like, add a blueberry, some toasted coconut, or more whipped cream on top of each dessert.

Nutrition: 172 cals; fat 2.1g; chole 1.4mg; sodium 349.6mg; carbs 34.8g; protein 4.7g.

CHERRY CREAM CHEESE DESSERT

Preparation time: 15 minute **Cooking time:** 30 minutes **Servings:** 4

Ingredients:

- 1 cup of crushed shortbread cookies
- 3 tbsp. unsalted butter, melted
- 1 tbsp. white sugar
- 1 (8 Oz.) package of reduced-fat cream cheese
- ½ cup of low-fat plain Greek yogurt
- ½ cup of sweetened condensed milk
- 2 tbsp. fresh lemon juice
- 1 tsp. almond extract
- 1 pinch salt
- 1 (21 Oz.) can of cherry pie filling

Directions:

Butter, sugar, and shortbread cookie crumbs are combined in a small bowl; set aside. Mix the cream cheese, yogurt, condensed milk, lemon juice, almond essence, and a little salt in a dish. Beat with an electric mixer until uniform. Four 8-Oz. canning jars or small dessert dishes should each have about 1 tbsp of the cookie batter in the bottom. Layers of the cream cheese mixture and cherry pie filling should be added using a spoon or piping bag. Continue stacking in this manner. Desserts should be placed in the refrigerator to chill for at least 30 minutes before serving.

Nutrition: 803 cals; protein 13.2g; carbs 106.8g; fat 35.8g; chole 79.1mg; sodium 541.5mg.

CONVERSION TABLES OF THE VARIOUS UNITS OF MEASUREMENT

COOKING CONVERSION CHART

Measurement

CUP	ONCES	MILLILITERS	TABLESPOONS
8 cup	64 oz	1895 ml	128
6 cup	48 oz	1420 ml	96
5 cup	40 oz	1180 ml	80
4 cup	32 oz	960 ml	64
2 cup	16 oz	480 ml	32
1 cup	8 oz	240 ml	16
3/4 cup	6 oz	177 ml	12
2/3 cup	5 oz	158 ml	11
1/2 cup	4 oz	118 ml	8
3/8 cup	3 oz	90 ml	6
1/3 cup	2.5 oz	79 ml	5.5
1/4 cup	2 oz	59 ml	4
1/8 cup	1 oz	30 ml	3
1/16 cup	1/2 oz	15 ml	1

Temperature

FAHRENHEIT	CELSIUS
100 °F	37 °C
150 °F	65 °C
200 °F	93 °C
250 °F	121 °C
300 °F	150 °C
325 °F	160 °C
350 °F	180 °C
375 °F	190 °C
400 °F	200 °C
425 °F	220 °C
450 °F	230 °C
500 °F	260 °C
525 °F	274 °C
550 °F	288 °C

Weight

IMPERIAL	METRIC
1/2 oz	15 g
1 oz	29 g
2 oz	57 g
3 oz	85 g
4 oz	113 g
5 oz	141 g
6 oz	170 g
8 oz	227 g
10 oz	283 g
12 oz	340 g
13 oz	369 g
14 oz	397 g
15 oz	425 g
1 lb	453 g

261

30 DAY MEAL PLAN

Days	Breakfast	Lunch	Dinner	Dessert/Snack
1	Home-Fried Breakfast Potatoes	Anti-Inflammatory Beef Meatballs	Sesame Couscous Chicken	Chocolate Beet Cake
2	Apple-Tahini Toast	Salmon with Veggies Sheet Pan	Fire-Roasted Tomatoes Over Chicken	Dijon Roasted Asparagus
3	Oatmeal Cookies	Roasted Salmon	Bunless Sloppy Joes	Strawberry Pie

		Garlic and Broccoli		
4	Cheesy Bacon Casserole	Roasted Sweet Potatoes with Avocado Dip	Beef Curry	Paprika Tofu & Zucchini Skewers
5	Mexican-Style Breakfast Casserole	Chicken with Lemon and Asparagus	Asian Grilled Beef Salad	Grape Skillet Galette
6	Banana Pancakes With Apricots	Apple Squash Soup	Mustard Glazed Pork Chops	Chocolate Bars with Walnuts
7	Pudding With Blackcurrant And Mint	Quick Pumpkin Soup	Parmesan-Crusted Pork Chops	Tapioca Pudding
8	Quinoa Bread With Pecan Walnut Butter	Chicken Squash Soup	Cherry-Glazed Lamb Chops	Apple and Cinnamon Chips
9	Oat Flakes With Pears And Blueberries	Healthy Broccoli Soup	Lamb and Vegetable Stew	Mango Mug Cake
10	Soy Cream With Asparagus	Asian Chicken	Lemon-Pepper Tilapia	Celery with Curry Sauce

		Coconut Soup		
11	Sweet Potato Hash	Mashed Grape Tomato Pizzas	Rosemary Lamb Chops	Honey Stewed Apples
12	Salmon Egg Scrambled	Greek Vegetable Salad Pita	Roasted Pork Loin	Skewers of Tofu And Zucchini
13	Chia Chocolate Pudding	Burgers	Chicken Chili	Apricot Cake
14	Baked Oatmeal	Brown Rice with Bell Peppers	Chicken Vera Cruz	Crisps Made From Sweet Potato
15	Creamy Smoothie Bowl	Bean and Rice Casserole	Chicken and Cornmeal Dumplings	Pumpkin And Dates Cake
16	Mediterranea n Eggs	Herby Quinoa with Walnuts	Gazpacho	Sticks With Sesame And Turmeric
17	Cauliflower Breakfast Porridge	Chipotle Kidney Bean Chili	Tomato and Kale Soup	Mint Chocolates
18	Almond Flour Pancakes with Strawberries	Southern Bean Bowl	Squash Soup with Crispy Chickpeas	Quinoa and Lemon Cookies

19	Pistachio And Pecan Walnuts Granola	Cream of Corn Soup	Vegetarian Chili	Peanut Butter and Chocolate Balls
20	Banana Muffin	Cabbage Beef Borscht	Italian Style Eggplant Casserole	Apple and Cinnamon Chips
21	Mushroom Frittata	Lemon Pepper Beef Soup	Veggie-Stuffed Burritos	Spiced Sweet Pecans
22	Spicy Quinoa	Cream of Crab Soup	Artichoke Quiche	Chocolate Beet Cake
23	Tofu Scramble	Crab and Shrimp Gumbo	Blue Cheese Field Salad	Greek Yogurt Affogato with Pistachios
24	Anti-inflammatory Porridge	Pearl Barley And Red Beans Soup	Spicy Asparagus-Tempeh	Strawberry Pie
25	Gingerbread Oatmeal	Soup Of Mushrooms And Tempeh	Veggie Cheddar Frittata	Dessert Crepes
26	Roasted Almonds	Cauliflower And Miso Soup	Spinach Alfredo Lasagna	Grape Skillet Galette
27	Roasted Pumpkin Seeds	Asparagus And Tamari Soup	Vegetable Minestrone Soup	Lemon Pineapple Dessert

28	Quick Burrito	Oven Beef Stew	Vegan Chili with White Bean	Apricot Cake
29	Nutty Choco-Nana Pancakes	Harvest Beef Stew	Cauliflower Fried Rice	Cherry Cream Cheese Dessert
30	Blueberry Avocado Chocolate Muffins	Beef and Vegetable Stew	Asparagus Pita Rounds	Peanut Butter and Chocolate Balls

Printed in Great Britain
by Amazon

48861631R00156